MARIE LENÔTRE

Appetites

A MEMOIR

bright sky press

HOUSTON, TEXAS

The author has dedicated proceeds
from the sale of this book to the
Gaston LeNôtre Scholarship Foundation.

bright sky press
HOUSTON, TEXAS

2365 Rice Blvd., Suite 202
Houston, Texas 77005

ISBN: 978-1-939055-90-3

10   9   8   7   6   5   4   3   2   1

Library of Congress Cataloging-in-Publication Data on file with publisher.

appetitesbymarielenotre.com

Editorial Direction: Lucy Herring Chambers
Designer: Marla Y. Garcia

Printed in Canada through Friesens

To my mother, Αικατερίνη Χομπιτη, whom I love and know more since reading about Greece in World War II and the subsequent Civil War.

In Gratitude

I am grateful for the spirit in me which ignites my breath and captures the splendor of the universe at every moment.

I am grateful for my husband who saved me from drowning and continues to support me in every step I take.

I am grateful for my three children: Nathalie, who is a caring doctor, a loving mother to Amélie and wife to Paul, and who has accompanied me through my pains and gains since she was a young adult and brought me joy and enthusiasm for all that I do; Armelle, who is a proud mother of Sophie and Max and a loving wife to Malcolm, who continues to pursue her interests in science education and in policy and never ceases to show me affection and interest in my work and studies; and Gaston, who is father of baby Bernard and Beatrice, who with his wife Kate is committed to the universal truth and goodness and is able to recognize this in me.

I am grateful for my three Greek sisters Neny, Athena, and Elda, for their unconditional love and encouragement.

I am grateful to writer John DeMers and Lucy Chambers from Bright Sky Press. Without John and Lucy this book could not have been started or completed. John helped me put words where I could not and Lucy provided inestimable editorial advice and insights. I also want to give heartfelt thanks to Kate LeNôtre, Nathalie Schulhof and Armelle Casau who assisted me in polishing the final text.

I am grateful to all my friends listed at *www. GastonLenotreScholarship.org.* I have marveled at their generosity and genuine friendship. Their support to the Gaston LeNôtre Scholarship and its Endowment Fund is an enormous encouragement for me to go forward.

Special thanks go to Gaston LeNôtre Scholarship Board of Directors, Paula Sutton, James Crump, Dennis Steger, Randy Fournier, Joana Tagaropulos, Debbie Woehler, Bob Cress, and Connie Valerius for their faithful commitment.

I am grateful to the Advisory Board of the Culinary Institute LeNôtre: Charles Carroll at the helm, Fritz Gitschner, Thomas Preuml, Diane D'Agostino, Claire Smith, Ernie Pekmezaris, Mary Grace Gray, and Randy Fournier, for their guidance and professional leadership; and to Les Dames d'Escoffier Organization where I served two years as president and who continue to support my work and the school.

I am grateful to these friends who have generously served our fundraising Champagne & Chocolat Scholarship Gala from 2001 to 2014 as Chairs, Honorary Chairs, and Honorees:

Chairs: Steve Payne, Eddie Lewis, Lucia and Michael Cordua, Paula Sutton and Bill Gross, Thomas and Deborah Woehler, Bill King, Philamena and Arthur Baird, Melissa Edwards, Stephanie and Paul Madan, Katina and Monty McDannald, Jane-Page and James Crump, Kaye Horn, Janine Jannarelli, and Tina Raham Stewart.

Honorary Chairs: Carolyn Farb, Tony Vallone, John DeMers, Dennis Steger, Diane and Jim D'Agostino, Marian and Harry Tindall, French Ambassador to the United States Jean-David Levitte, Jane-Page Crump, Consul General of France and Madame Frederic Bontemps, Deana and Larry Blackburn, Margaret Alek Williams, and Rolanette and Berdon Lawrence.

Honorees: Damian Mandola, Stan Holt, Audrey Holt, Kiran Verma, Teresa Byrne-Dodge, Fritz Gitschner, Charles Carroll, Cleverley Stone, Randy Fournier, Daniel Boulud, Dennis Steger, Jane-Page Crump, Paula Sutton, Helen and John Burris.

I am grateful to our students and instructors who volunteered the last fifteen years to raise money for the Gaston LeNôtre Scholarship Fund Gala to enable other students to fulfill their dreams.

I am grateful to our school associates, now all stockholders and the adjunct faculty less visible and yet oh-so-necessary for the academic and hospitality management courses. It takes a team to create anything, and the Culinary Institute LeNôtre could not be what it is today without their dedication, patience, work, and loyalty.

I am grateful to all Culinary Institute LeNôtre alumni and current students, who come from the five continents, remote villages, small cities, and big cities. It takes courage, work, and determination to improve oneself. Ultimately it is for the good and the betterment of humanity for which we are all striving.

Special thanks and recognition goes to Charles Carroll, whose book, *Tasting Success* written for aspiring chefs and sold in our school bookstore, inspired me to write mine.

I am thankful to all of you for walking alongside me on this journey. The love I found in me is the love you have sent me!

www.culinaryinstitute.edu
mlenotre@culinaryinstitute.edu

Appetites

A MEMOIR

The recipe for life calls for ingredients, pots, pans, and... a continually hot oven.

CALEB SCHARF

Prologue

I spend most of the year in our cooking school. My office is in the North Campus of our 38,000 square-foot laboratory building with six cooking labs, six pastry and baking labs, a student refectory and a public restaurant. We are cooking and baking from eight in the morning until ten at night. We—that is our students, chefs, staff, guests and visitors—eat what we cook and bake. The aromas of freshly baked croissants, brioches and breads, *pot au feu*, bourguignon, roast lamb, or *moules marinière* permeate my office and escape from the walls into our parking lot.

You might wonder what my secret is, staying slim amid abundant gorgeous food. It is simple: Growing up, I learned from my father to eat out of sheer pleasure and reverence for the gift of life, and not out of frustration, or to fill a void in my heart. Because when you think of it, food is sacred. To live, we have to kill something that is alive—either vegetable or animal—and eat it. So I always pray before a meal and give thanks for my good fortune. Yes, I respect food as sacred.

I wrote this memoir with my husband Alain at my side. He cared about me completing my work. During the years in Houston when I was furthering my education, he loved to be involved, to learn what I did, to discuss and comment on my readings, and to read my writings. Now, Alain is co-author of my story. He became so passionately enamored of my endeavor, telling me his own story, editing the manuscript, selecting my poems. Our lives are so intertwined and—although I went into a fifteen-year education spree to be independently minded, educate myself in all I was lacking, and to someday become somebody in my own right—I find myself still so closely connected to Alain. He is my shadow that validates my persona.

Our children, our friends and supporters, our Culinary Institute LeNôtre and its students, the Gaston LeNôtre Scholarship Charity, and now this book, are my labor of love, reflecting my commitment and esteem for those with whom I share this life. I feel blessed all over.

But it has not always been that way.

I am not a chef.

I married a chef, a family of chefs, and my life changed dramatically.

Contents

I am thirteen years old here.

CHAPTER 1

What A Bottle You Threw Into The Sea

The meeting of two personalities is like the contact of two chemical substances: if there is any reaction, both are transformed.

CARL JUNG

It was Paris 1980. But it certainly wasn't the legendary April in Paris of song and movies I had experienced as a young woman. In fact, it was January, and more days than not were cold and rainy. After my divorce from my first husband, I had recently moved from my beautiful house in southwest France, into a small apartment in Paris. I'd even more recently sent my two daughters, ages seven and five, to live with my ex-husband and the woman he lived with then. I was new (again) in Paris, and I was new (again) in my travel agency job—where all my coworkers kept assuring me I was young, pretty and ought to be going out and being happy. No, what they actually said was I should be having fun, which always meant something involving men. And it was only beginning to dawn on me that, as much as I liked waking up next to a man each morning, the thought of it being a different man each morning was not appealing. Every day I thought of the fun they wanted me to have, it made me more miserable than it had the day before.

There's something depressing about not feeling romantic in what most people consider the most romantic city on earth. You feel a lot lonelier than you might anywhere else, just looking at all those people, kissing on the benches along the Seine River, holding hands, smiling into each other's bright eyes. Their palpable connection made me desperately sad, and missing my daughters made it even worse.

"They'll be fine," my ex assured me, no doubt gazing out at splashes of Provencal sunshine that made a cruel joke of Paris' gray, wintry skies. Cezanne lived and painted in those sunny splashes, the wild passions of Van Gogh still animated the area. I had lived there, too, yet all such things, such feelings, lived only in my past, if indeed they had ever lived for me. "You have a new job," my ex said, "and you'll have to travel some, and here they have everything they need. Miti—yes, that was the other woman's name—is taking such good care of them. The girls can go back home with you when you get settled. For good."

Right, I wanted to snarl. Michelle, Miti, that woman, she was single with a dog, I had never met her and never wished to! Who knows what she was concocting, trying to steal my dear daughters from me because she had no children of her own. My apartment was empty and silent, Paris beyond the windows empty and silent too, as though everything I carried inside me was slowly destroying everything outside, devouring all the light and color that should have been part of my life.

When I felt like making the effort, I tried to look on the bright side. I had an apartment in one of the liveliest neighborhoods on the Right Bank of Paris, sharing the famous 9th arrondissement with what locals called the Grands Boulevards designed by Baron Haussmann during France's Second Empire, with the "wedding cake" of an opera house designed by Charles Garnier and home to the Phantom of the Opera, and even with two of the city's best known department stores, Galleries Lafayette and Printemps. Just a quick stroll away was the Olympia concert hall, where everybody from Edith Piaf to the young Beatles had performed, and also the Hotel Scribe, where the appropriately named Lumière brothers had staged the world's first public film screening in 1895. The fact that movies had played such a role in my life up to this point that this particular bit of Paris history struck me as bittersweet, at best.

My former husband had not wanted to marry in the first place, so why would he want to bother with the formality of divorce now? In France, keeping a wife was a sure thing—many men who indulged in affairs or even kept long-time mistresses still called their wives their "rock." And some married women I'd known, both in my homeland of Greece and in my adopted country of France, didn't understand why I wanted out.

But I wanted out. I'd consulted a lawyer, decided I would keep the house, the car, and my daughters. I was trying to figure out what my options were, hoping at the same time that my husband would miss me so much he would return to me, would—as upside down as I knew the words were—take me back. But he did not. He did not want to relinquish the other woman, and he did not want to divorce me either. Perfect, I decreed at last. I sold our house quickly, moved back to Paris, and in a week found an apartment just blocks from the Opera.

I also found a job. I had always loved to travel, had worked at Olympic Airways for two years, and loved the idea of seeing the world, so Athens Tours Travel Agency seemed a perfect fit. What's more, our specialty was travel between Paris and Athens—a route made popular, even beyond regular vacation and business, by the number of Greek expats living in Paris. Within a short time, my fluency in Greek, French and English helped me climb the agency ladder, and I was also regularly asked to liaison in person with our Athens office.

It was the eighties, and that meant learning yet another foreign language—computers. They intrigued me, and, over time, I mastered the techniques of programming our (now primitive) computer systems, inputting data about flights, schedules, pricing and hotels, and generally being the go-to person in our company for all-things-tech. No one could have been more surprised by this aptitude than I was.

Yet, even that validation at work did not make me happy. With my daughters gone to their father (so I could concentrate), nothing made me happy. Finally, after several co-workers had tried and failed to make me go out on dates and have fun—my ex-mother-in-law (of all people) came up with an idea. She said I should place a personal ad in a magazine. I was horrified. Surely nobody I knew would do such a thing, I assured her—until she told me that was how she'd found her husband.

My childhood in Athens, Greece, had been all about my looks. Beauty contests, theater and movie roles had not provided a comfortable space for me, but they had led me to believe that finding a partner should not be such a challenge. After making my peace with the idea of looking for a man this way, I wrote some copy that started with a single word, the international distress signal "SOS." And I continued:

"Excellent upbringing, 35 years old, professional situation, divorced, blonde, charming, blue eyes, slim, pretty, own apartment and car, 5'5", educated, classy, sincere, would marry man 35-45 years, distinguished, intelligent, generous, good humored, wealthy. *Merci!*"

Sincere though I was, I left out that I had two daughters— the very daughters I was missing almost more than I could bear. Within a couple of weeks, technology being what it was back then, I'd received 150 letters from men hoping to be my mate. I found them boring, which made me even more depressed. Most of the men had children of their own that they wanted me to take care of, while others simply wanted me to take care of them. Many presented themselves as educated and successful, and they probably were, but none of them made the whole idea of being with somebody seem right. I spent nights reading these letters and crying. It was obvious that all these men were simply not for me.

And then…after a week with no letters, there was one small envelope that came through the mail. A one page letter, the only one I had received with a photo attached, with even the name and address on the upper left side. It began: "Young lady, what a bottle you threw into the sea! Was your divorce a shipwreck? Mine certainly was a big storm I would not wish it upon anyone." The letter made the promise of "sincere and loyal intentions as to your future."

This man wrote that he sailed. I suppose he liked to travel, and the photo he enclosed seemed to confirm all that he said. He was dressed in a jacket and tie as though for the office. He had an affectionate smile. And while I thought he was handsome, there was nothing of what I'd call the actor about him. I'd had more than my fill of them by the time I was twenty-one. This man and his letter seemed different from the others. I slept with the letter and waited until the next day to call him, agreeing to have lunch that Sunday. Alain LeNôtre, the letter said. I noted the first name, naturally, since that was the name of my ex-husband. The family name "LeNôtre" meant nothing to me at all.

We met in front of my apartment at noon. Once inside his car, I noticed there was an elegant Irish Setter quietly filling the entire back seat; Alain said the setter belonged to his father. I also noticed a smell that wasn't the least bit doggy: freshly baked croissants and bread. Really, it would be hard for anybody to complain about that. But I was a bit scared of the dog, which did not bark or even budge.

Over lunch—at a very fancy restaurant called Pavillon du Lac, among the well-manicured greenery of the Bois de Boulogne— we talked about ourselves, our lives, our jobs, like any man and woman on a first date. Alain started us out with a bottle of *Champagne*—Laurent Perrier Grand Siècle it read—and an order of seared *foie gras*. He was French, after all, and the menu went onward and upward from there. By course three, I understood that his family owned a different fancy restaurant in the Bois de Boulogne, one called Pré Catelan, but that he hadn't wanted to take me there on our first date. His family was, he let on, a bit famous in Paris, especially for catering and pastries, and not only his father but his grandfather and even grandmother had been respected French chefs in the 1900s.

By the time lunch was winding down, and we had a promenade on the lake with the setter (who was adorable), Alain asked
me if I'd have dinner with him that night. "I have to go somewhere for work," he explained, "and I'd love for you to go with
me." He drove me home, was very polite upon parting, and returned several hours later after I'd changed to go to dinner at no
less a place than the famous Paradis Latin. Now that was a place
I'd heard of.

At this hottest, hippest, most desirable cabaret in Paris, celebrities from French politics, sports and entertainment competed
to get tables every night of the year. I wasn't sure I quite measured
up, since so many of the women arrived wearing mink coats and
nearly all the men, including Alain, were dressed in tuxedos. We
got a table easily, though, in a private lounge! We had dinner
with champagne again as we watched the show. Alain was calm
the entire time, though he did occasionally check his watch or
look around to see what might be happening next. It was, he
explained to me eventually, the famous club owner's birthday—
and it was time for him to go to work. Politely, he excused himself from our table, and disappeared.

As I sat alone, the entertainers, including dozens of statu-
esque showgirls, cleared the stage. And then there was the very
famous Jean Marie Rivière, nightclub owner, in the spotlight. A
huge birthday cake appeared from backstage, wheeled out by no
less than Gaston LeNôtre himself (although I would later learn
it was Gaston's brother Marcel, who often stood in since they
looked so much alike) and my date, Alain LeNôtre. With the
backstage efficiency of a showgirl, he had transformed himself,
and was now resplendent in a pristine chef's jacket with a *toque
blanche* towering above his head.

Even as I sat watching Alain nod rather shyly to all the ap-
plause—and yes, even as a nubile showgirl popped out of the top
of that birthday cake—I caught myself thinking of his letter. He
was the only man out of 150 who actually understood my ad. He
was certainly the only one who said, in word and now in his gal-
lant actions: I'm here to save you from drowning!

At age ten, with my teacher and classmates in Agia Paraskevi elementary school

CHAPTER 2

War & Miracles

*We are not human beings
having a spiritual experience,
we are spiritual beings having
a human experience.*

TEILHARD DE CHARDIN

From the Age of Pericles on, there have been
both golden and challenging times to be born
in Greece. I was born in one of the more difficult periods. Between my arrival in 1944 and 1949, Greece struggled not
only with World War II but also with our own piece of the Cold
War, the Greek civil war. Because of communist infiltrations from
Albania and Yugoslavia, backed by Soviet Union and Bulgaria,
the civil war was Greek vs. Greek, and that produced some of the
worst bloodlettings ever.

Both my parents had their roots on the island of Crete, known
now as the home of Zorba and a place of rugged beauty. Yet,
Crete is also a place of fierce independence. Life there tended to
be dark and violent, full of the kind of vendettas that Americans
always associate with Sicily. My mother's parents migrated to
America to flee such a problem and settled in New York City
where my mother was born in 1920. She was their only child. She
grew up as an American, staying there until she was ten. But the

Great Depression quickly pushed her family out, and they went back to Athens, where it was generally safer to live—until the wars broke out and gave my father something to grieve for the rest of his life.

Not long before my birth, World War II produced two quite different invasions of my homeland. The first was attempted by the Italians, who at the time had joined with the Nazis as one of the Axis powers. Mussolini's armies moved through Albania into the mountains of northern Greece in 1940 and, even though many had experience with mountains before, they were impotent against Greeks who not only knew the mountain terrain intimately, but also were fighting for their country. It was brutal fighting, but eventually the Italians gave up and retreated.

Not so the Germans, who invaded Greece in April 1941 through Bulgaria and Yugoslavia. At the start, Greek freedom fighters declared that Greece would never be occupied by Nazis. But the greater numbers and the more powerful war machine took their toll. Eventually we were occupied. My father, I would learn much later because of his reluctance to boast, had served heroically. When he came back home from the icy mountains of Epirus his garments were flea-infested rags which my mother burned on the spot. The Greek war prime minister, who ran a fascist government, negotiated to surrender, under two conditions: One was not to surrender to the Italians they had beaten, and the other was for the Greek soldiers to return home. This they did, even though many ended up facing starvation.

The economy had collapsed, and there were no jobs for the returning soldiers. The Germans, Italians, and Bulgarians occupying Greece had forbidden the trade of food between Greek provinces. The Allies had placed an embargo on food sales to the Axis conquests—in time of peace, one third of the food was imported. The occupation armies looted the food and burned the harvest, as reprisal against the resistance. Three hundred thousand Greeks died of hunger, forty thousand in Athens alone. My mother even sold her jewelry for bread, oil, beans, and butter to get us some protein. Others, less fortunate, sold all their belongings, even their houses, in exchange for food to survive. Many Athenians who were left with nothing to sell were found each morning, sheer skeletons, and discarded from the city.

As World War II wound down toward Germany's surrender, an event occurred that changed my family forever. One day, my father's younger and only brother, who was part of the Cretan resistance, was walking along a road in his village in Crete, carrying two rifles to show off to his fellow villagers. He was suddenly confronted by a German soldier, who ordered the seventeen-year-old to stop and disarm. The young man, who would have become my uncle, no doubt felt the defiance of generations. He refused to give up his guns and continued walking down the street. He even asked why he should obey, since the Nazis were obviously finished anyway. The German soldier shot him dead. My father's father died within a year, never having escaped from his wrenching grief, and my grandmother died a year later.

As a result, I never met my paternal grandparents. By all accounts, my father was never the same either, and he never put his foot on Cretan soil again. Years later, they would send me to our paternal village for summer vacations with an uncle and an aunt who treated me as their own since they were unable to have children themselves. In the village, I could play wild games with my cousin Sifi—we were the same age—running everywhere among the boulders and ravines with no fear that my mother would come after me. But, back to the war years...

The end of one conflict signaled the beginning of another, and for us in Greece, the next was even worse. There were, as usual in our country, old scores to settle—plus an issue we were obviously incapable of settling: the role of communism in our future. By the time I was four, the shouting had turned into shooting and the Greek civil war was at its worst. I am not clear on what I actually remember, as opposed to what I remember being told, but I will never forget my mother's tales of our family escaping Athens on foot, leaving our house to the violent bands of communist men who would sweep through taking food, clothing, jewelry, and any guns or knives they could find. We hid in the hills at a relative's home, until the British troops sent by Churchill liberated Athens. Then we returned to our home and tried to live some kind of life. Not a normal life, just some kind of life.

The unsteady peace that followed was filled with resentment, guilt and grueling austerity. When the British came to our rescue in 1949, it was natural for my mother to volunteer her language skills. She served as a translator between the British and the Greeks, who managed to fabricate soles for their shoes out of cut up old jeep tires. The British gave us military blankets, sweaters and coats, cans of food, milk and chocolate.

We had little in the way of luxury, even though my father had a good job as an executive for the Bank of Greece, good enough to provide the basics for my parents and all four of the daughters they would eventually have. As best as I can recall, I had no toys except one small doll that wore a pale pink dress—nothing like the closets full of toys so many boys and girls have now. On Christmas, my sisters and I did not find our gifts under the branches of the tree, but hanging on them. Peeling the oranges we found tucked in the boughs was all the unwrapping we did, but we were happy just to have a tree and oranges and mandarins from our garden. We did not know anything better. And we were given tickets for our daily bread. My older sister Neny or the maid had to go and stand in line for that. Everything else we had to eat was something we had to search for or bargain to obtain.

This was not the glory that was Greece. It was all the Greece that was left after nearly a decade of two horrific wars and, before that, more than four hundred years of Turkish occupation. We were now a poor country, and it was a struggle to recover from all that we had been through. No matter how diminished our fortunes, though, whenever our freedom was at risk, we Greeks would rise and fight to the death.

But, even though I came into this world in austere times, our neighborhood and indeed my life were fairly affluent by the standards of the day. We lived in a four-bedroom one-story house that had a basement and an upper floor for storage and laundry, plus a terrace above that. A large patio covered with vines led to a vegetable garden in one corner and further down a place for chickens. I never ventured that way, as I never liked the sight of chickens. There was also a garden with lemon trees, mandarin trees, and flowers and roses all around the wall fence. You give a Greek anything resembling a terrace, no matter how small, no matter how crumbling with age or neglect, and he will find a way to reach the sunshine. Maybe we all grew up with the dream of Icarus. Maybe we're all in danger of flying too close to the sun.

That terrace was the scene of my earliest theatrical performances. There were usually sheets hanging from a clothesline to dry, and I made those my very first theater curtains. My younger sister, Athena, was often by my side, and she helped with the props. Using mother's shoes and robes, I played among those hanging sheets, so pure and white—and so unlike the theater world I would come to know—proclaiming my lines with enthusiasm, pretending to laugh or cry or sometimes die. From a very young age, I started to think of my life in terms of pretending.

Some things that took place on this terrace were all too real. My brave and insolent sister Neny who was four years older than I was, never tired of hearing what our mother told her and then doing the exact opposite. How jealous I was, and how much more impressed I became in adolescence, at her sheer audacity and confidence. Neny was always up to some mischief, whether it was screaming rude comments at other people's maids as they walked along the sidewalk below or even dumping our maid's cleaning water on the heads of nicely dressed people. Our mother certainly got an earful about that.

The same obstinacy seemed to be behind my sister's academic performance, which started out impressive enough to win a scholarship to the American school and went not just downhill but over a cliff after that. Our mother started beating Neny with the iron ruler we used to do our homework, and I watched the terrifying scenes from behind the sofa. With the survival instinct of a small child, I knew what to do to avoid the same pain: always be cautious; always do what mother says. The only time I managed to make my mother furious, she came at me with a coat hanger. I escaped and hid in the laundry room upstairs for the entire day, emerging only after her anger had subsided.

Separating myself from my sister Neny in another way, I also learned to always go to church and always pray—two things Neny was proudest of never doing. There was a time when I prayed to God virtually around the clock, and I anticipated the weekly walk to church with my father each Sunday morning with longing. Our Greek Orthodox Church of Agios Ioannis—St. John—always smelled of eucalyptus which lined the majestic front courtyard. It also smelled from the incense and the flickering candles that people lined up to buy before entering. Dark and humid, the church was filled with worshippers crossing themselves and bowing their heads beneath a golden flourish of icons and the overarching figure of Jesus, known as the Pantocrator, that covered the soaring dome.

My father believed firmly in God and called on him in all situations. I therefore had created a relationship with God deep inside me, as well. I talked to this entity as a friend but without making any human representation. God was up there somewhere and I was down below talking to him, expecting and believing he was listening to me with compassion. I went to catechism classes every Sunday after Mass and relished the stories of Jesus and his miracles.

If God did miracles, he could do anything. So, later in middle school having not studied enough for my theology class exam and always expecting A's, of course, I panicked—but not for long. I opened my book randomly, praying to God that the page would be the subject for the exam. I learned that page by heart. And next day, that was exactly the subject of the exam. A miracle, I decided it was, and this reinforced my faith. I never dared to admit to anyone that I talked with God and that he listened to me. It was my secret, and it made me feel special in a way. But for nothing in the world would I take advantage of such privilege, and I used it only in emergencies.

My personality formed early, before I gave it any thought. From the age of three, everything needed to be perfect for me, from the embroidered sheets on my bed to the pink or blue ribbons and bows I'd attach to my little brown purse. Neny, Athena, and I were always neatly dressed and pretty, with well-chosen outfits, handbags and shoes. Our neighbors liked to call us "the little sirens," an innocent moniker which they meant simply as beautiful girls. In later years, the image darkened for me when I learned that sirens were heartless creatures who lured men and their ships to crash upon the rocks.

Despite my passion for the nicest things money could buy, I also had a wild side—many young girls do, I suppose. When I was five, I first went to spend the summer with aunts and uncles on the island of Crete. It was a different world, filled with nature, adventure, and discoveries far removed from my peaceful and familiar neighborhood in the city. My father's village was called Rodakinon, which means peach because of the shape of the land, and I spent every waking minute with my cousins, all of whom were boys. By the end of the summer, I was talking back, running, jumping, and climbing over anything that stood still long enough, and I had the bumps, scrapes and bruises to prove it. I felt free. It didn't take my mother long to pull me back into line.

The postwar austerity of my childhood propelled me toward my life's first big dream—or at least toward my mother's first big dream for me. What we did, she and I, was go to the movies at the theater or in open-air theaters during the summer. That meant American movies, and that meant musicals in color. These were happy, escapist musicals of the sort America loved (and exported to the world) throughout the 50s and 60s.

Born in New York, my mother loved these musicals: pink and blue, full of idyllic songs, fluffy long dresses, and happy endings. She detested the black and white Greek movies, all about melodramatic love and war. "American actresses are so glamorous, so blond," she would say. "They sing, dance, and smile! I just love America." She was missing all things American. I am sure she dreamed of me becoming a movie star. And at times it looked as though she might get her wish. I was pretty and I was blonde— two things that most of the American girls on the big screen were at that time.

When the natural blond of my hair started to fade away at age twelve, once a month or so, my mother made me sit on a little stool in the bathroom. She would part my blond hair and dampen the dark roots with a piece of cotton that smelled of peroxide. "You were born a blond and must stay blond, sweetheart," she said, concentrating on her work, pushing my head down. "Blondes are pretty." My scalp stung, and I had to sit there, the cold cotton rubbing out my brain. Dear God, I wondered, why did I have to be blond like a white lamb? Nobody else in my school was blonde. I sensed that difference in the way some girls sneered at me behind my back. They hadn't liked me initially because of my hair. I didn't belong to the group, and my feelings of alienation made me stiff and cranky. I had to hold my head up not to cry, which made me look proud and even less likable, I'm sure. They called me "the iceberg." My mother didn't know that.

School was important to her. She paid for French lessons, English lessons, ballet, and piano. Each time I asked a question, she took out the big encyclopedia from the library. Solemnly, pulling her curly hair away from her face, she would read aloud the explanation. After she shared the answer with me, she continued reading silently, absorbed in the pages. When she walked around the house, she swayed with charm and grace, smiling, playing with her arms, her shoulders, her hips, her eyelashes, much like an ingénue in a Charlie Chaplin film. Gazing at her from behind the newspaper, his blue eyes wide open under his spectacles, my fair-haired father mumbled, "Brunette and tasty as honey-dew-sweet."

Whenever I got the flu, my mother rubbed my back with alcohol and mint, a long caress which warmed my flesh and cooled my brain. Then she fed me hot chicken *bouillon*, bits of tender chicken and angel hair pasta, sprinkled with fresh parsley and lemon. And the next day, she cooked lamb casserole for me, steamed rack of lamb with artichokes and pearly onions bathing in a creamy white sauce.

Some of her remedies were not so palatable. Every morning before breakfast I had to swallow a spoon full of cod liver oil.

She whipped our milk in a big glass with a raw egg. It formed a yellowish crust on the top. "It is more fortifying that way," my mother said. If I got the chance, I threw the repulsive mixture into the sink and quickly washed away the white foam. One day I rushed to school, forgetting to throw the milk into the sink. Sure enough, our nanny Athena (a popular Greek name then) who was in charge of carrying out my mother's inflexible orders, ran after me with the horrid concoction and made me drink it in front of the entire class, who watched in bewilderment. Athena's tiny brown eyes, red-rimmed from the run, cried victory. Fighting back tears, I yearned secretly for revenge.

My mother's passion was healthy food. Before dinner time, she cut thin sticks of raw carrots or celery, quarters of grapefruit, and shared them with me. "There are plenty of good vitamins in there." She devoured each bite. Afterwards, she hummed radio hits. I hated that singing. So happy and detached she looked then, as if she were not my mother at all but a star from one of these American musicals she was so fond of. The moments I despised most were when she had a telephone chat with Anthoula, her best friend, who talked constantly. Planted in the art-deco armchair of the living-room, next to the telephone table, my mother chatted and laughed about things and people I didn't know for what seemed to me endless hours. It was as if she had her own private life, and I was estranged from it all.

When I was about ten years old, my family moved to Agia Paraskevi, close to Mount Ymittos, a few kilometers away from downtown Athens. The air was always cooler and smelled of pine trees. Villas, girdled by gardens, had yellow, red, or white rosebushes, and apricot, fig, and pistachio trees. Walking to the school each day, I passed by a pistachio tree and I had to restrain myself from eating too many of the fresh pistachios: They have a reddish perfumed skin, a fruity green soft seed, and taste much better than the salted and grilled ones sold to the tourists.

My very first brush with the movie business came when I was thirteen, and it produced one of the central traumas of my entire life. My mother had entered me in a beauty contest to choose the Queen of the Spring in an open-air theater called the Amaryllis. I'd already started growing a woman's figure, a development not lost on any man looking at my low-cut turquoise dress.

The master of ceremonies, a stocky little man, perspired profusely under the stage lights. "Come on, girls," he kept admonishing us. "Don't be bashful." I didn't want to go, but my mother gave me a shove. I thought the contest, or any form of beauty contest, was ridiculous, but at thirteen, all I really cared about was pleasing my mother. Before long, I heard the crowd shouting its approval of my appearance—"The blonde, the blonde, the blonde!" I won the contest unanimously that day. I also caught the eye of an older man—what man isn't older when you're thirteen—who approached my mother about letting me take a small part in a film he was making.

"I'm extremely interested in your daughter," he said. "She has a rare beauty. Would you agree? My name is Sotiropulos. Pleased to meet you!"

"Oh, I'm flattered," my mother responded. "It's true, everyone compliments me about her. A film, you say? You want her to be in a movie? You don't think she's a little young?"

"Rest assured," he said. "It's the role of a young girl."

And indeed, two months later, I was chaperoned by my sister Neny, as we took a taxi to Kifisia, an affluent suburb nested in a lush greenery and palm trees with old mansions, in one of which the shooting was taking place. I was playing the role of a granddaughter of a countess, who at the end of her life tells her story through a photo album. Sotiropulos was lovely with me, directing the scene. I felt comfortable. During a break, Neny and I sat still on a rock and observed from a distance Sotiropulos and his five-crew staff filming the verandah of the chateau. He moved swiftly, giving multiple directions, gesturing, slipping behind the camera, and then jostling back, his arms up in the air. The camera swept around, the huge spot lights at work despite the bright hot sun, all together made a lavish ballet of men, machines, and nature.

Sotiropulos introduced me to the crew, all young men. They smiled at me, somewhat shy. He also introduced me to the leading lady. She sat in a bamboo old-fashioned rocking chair on the verandah. Heavy make-up and dark lines smudged her face to make her appear older. We had sandwiches after the shooting and Sotiropulos told me that he would soon see me to prepare for the next film. Being an actress, I soon discovered, was easier and more fun than learning chemistry or Latin, and right then, I decided that this was something I could do.

One day, Sotiropulos showed up at our house to see me privately, and my mother received him well, offering chocolates and brandy, thrilled to hear that her daughter would be in another film soon.

This seemed to be all the reassurance my mother needed to let her thirteen-year-old daughter move into this man's world, the very world that always promised magic to her, that always sounded like the life anybody must want. Yet this "role of a lifetime" ended up being the nightmare of my lifetime. A couple of months later, when the director came by our house to take me to the movie studio, he took me instead to an apartment. To this day, I can't believe my mother didn't see this coming.

I did not like the director. He used so many big words and got so excited when he talked that I thought his eyes were going to pop out of his head. I thought he was stupid. In the apartment, first, under the guise of teaching me about my movie role, he forced a kiss on me. I hated it, but feeling I had no choice, I endured it. Then he made me undress while he watched and proceeded to touch me in places no one had ever touched me before. He did not try to have intercourse with me. I did not understand it at the time, but later I realized he was impotent. I felt violated and abused all the same.

"I want to go home, please," I protested finally, pushing him back and freeing myself.

"OK, all right, we'll go," he said, and I looked carefully at him for the first time, half-naked, white and flabby.

God, how ugly and old he was, and how submissive. I was surprised. I could have yelled sooner, had I known.

He put on his shirt and pants while I gathered my clothes and dressed hurriedly with a newly acquired resolve.

"You're not mad, are you?" he said, his hair hanging over his sweaty face.

"I just want to go home, *now*, that's all." My throat and mouth felt dry, and my heart thumped. With the back of my hand, I wiped away tears.

It certainly wasn't something I could talk with my mother about, and the handful of friends I felt I could confide in had little more wisdom than I. Many years later, after studying psychology, I finally began to understand what had happened to me. Writing about myself as "Anna," I found my way back to the dreadful weeks and months after that encounter. "Anna's personality changes radically," I wrote. "Guilt, unconscious hatred for men, and severe self-criticism develop rapidly. She loses her energy, self-confidence, and religious faith. She does poorly in school, and avoids communication with her family... Although she wants to be a doctor, she abandons that vocation. She has learned to be a victim and is incapable of any specific, high goals."

Indeed, things turned upside down for me after this. The rock that had been my faith collapsed in rubble. I felt abandoned— not betrayed, just simply left by myself, developing a feeling of unworthiness, and self-loathing. I was discovering a world that I found ugly, mean, repulsive. I was changing physically as well, getting a woman' s body. But inside, I was a frightened and wounded child.

Although I had my loving parents, two sisters I had grown up with, and now a third who was by then four years old, I felt isolated holding on to my terrible secret, pushing it down inside, pushing myself down as well. God suddenly went out of sight. I could not see him anywhere. It was as if the world had changed and there was no space for God. This void in my life continued for a long, long time, in fact until I met Alain LeNôtre, a genuinely practicing Catholic who drew me gently back to my faith and inner peace. With his encouragement, I renewed my love of attending church, especially the Greek Orthodox church. The sacred icons, painted bright blue, red and green all over the walls, the iconostasis and the ceiling, and the smell of the incense, all were old friends, long missed, that reminded me of my childhood. Today, when I feel disconnected, a deep long breath suffices to reassure me that all is well between me and God.

When I was fourteen, a year after the incident, a producer came to my school and announced he was shooting scenes there for yet another happy musical. He had made arrangements with the school director to use our school as a natural setting, and we received a notice asking if we students wanted to serve as extras. My best friend Anna volunteered and pushed me to do the same. "This will be so much fun," she said. There we were in a film shot in our very classroom, in lovely black and white.

Before the movie crew finished, the film director—Sakelarios was his name and he was quite famous—told me he wanted me in his next film. He asked me to get the permission of my parents, because we would have to go out on location for a week the following summer on the island of Poros. He said that I would even have a small speaking part. And, he added, the film would be shot in color, color being all the rage at that time. Oh, my mother was in heaven. We couldn't have known then that the two most beloved Greek movies of all time, *Never on Sunday* and *Zorba the Greek*, would both be shot and shown in black and white. My mother thought the chance for me to be in a color movie was well worth my going to Poros the summer of the following year.

The big day came fast, and I was presented to the film director immediately upon my arrival at the studios. Sakelarios was a short bald man, jovial and decent. He never tried anything with me, and so I could breathe freely, with nothing to fear. I loved being in this movie. The island was beautiful, and the people involved in the film were friendly. We ate breakfast, lunch and dinner together on the terrace, which was covered with grape vines and faced the still waters of the little port of Poros. Our quarters were bleached white houses with blue painted doors and shutters, facing the quiet turquoise water.

The whole experience felt exciting and romantic. Like the fifteen-year-old girl that I was, I fell madly in love with the leading man, Dimitri, who must have been twenty-seven or so. I found him so handsome, with his sky-blue eyes and an irresistible smile on his red lips. Luckily for me, Sakelarios put me right next to Dimitri during the scenes on board a two-mast sailing yacht. Between takes, the star and I joked lightly, as cameras and sound were set up or corrected around us. Bantering with a handsome movie star on a yacht certainly felt nice.

After dinner with the company one night, Dimitri extended his hand and asked me to go for a walk with him. Being Greek, he had to smoke a cigarette, though in those days nobody bothered to excuse themselves to smoke. I followed him like an automaton. We walked on the damp sand. He talked. He smoked. And all the while, it was dawning on me that we were moving farther from our friends, deeper and deeper into a thick grove of olive trees. Still naïve, it never occurred to me what would come next. Cigarette necessities dispensed with, my romantic leading man took me roughly into his arms and started kissing me, running his hands over my body. A crazy and desperate look came into his eyes.

"I want, I want you, baby," he said, moving to unzip his pants.

I struggled free and blurted out, "I'm a virgin!"

"What?" He stopped suddenly. "You're joking."

"It's true," I said.

Picking up his glasses, which had fallen during the tussle, he stumbled over his words, as he never did onscreen. "I didn't expect that," was all he could say. By this point, his hands had morphed from grappling me to trying to straighten his clothes. "Let's go back," he said, heading back down the beach.

"I'm sorry," I said, embarrassed and confused. He looked equally embarrassed, glancing at me with bewilderment, half smiling now.

"I would have never believed," he said. "What are you doing here?"

We stood in silence.

"Forgive me," he said finally.

I did not know how to respond, but I knew I had missed my big chance. As when we returned to the *taverna*, he acted as if nothing had happened, finishing his glass of wine, lighting a new cigarette, joking around with the crew.

I did not sleep that night. I cried to my best girlfriend on the set, but she couldn't help me. And I cried even more the next day as he did not talk to me, or ask me to go for a walk. I even started smoking to attract his attention, but he merely glanced at me occasionally with a brotherly smile, which left me feeling humiliated and rejected.

Back in Athens I cried and cried. My mother kept asking me what was the matter. I couldn't bring myself to tell her. I took up smoking for real. Sometimes I smoked and cried at the same time, listening with my eyes closed, to Dimitri's plays, broadcasted on the radio. What a curse to be a virgin, I thought to myself. Not surprisingly, that was the last film I was invited to do with that production company.

Alain at age three

CHAPTER 3

Born In Flour

Only the Best is good enough.
~GASTON LENÔTRE

I n the weeks, months and, of course, years
that followed my double-meal date with Alain
LeNôtre in Paris, I went from knowing nothing about
the name to knowing quite a bit about the family. He was born in
the French region of Normandy on Friday, April 13, 1945. If you
do the math, you realize that Gaston and Colette, his parents,
were feeling very friendly even as the Allied liberation of France,
that began with D-Day on the Normandy beaches, was going on
all around them. Nearly all of Alain's childhood would be a post-
battle scene from a war movie. Still, his birth only proves that
men and women will continue to be men and women, no matter
what else is happening. At least in France.

The LeNôtre family's roots were clearly in Normandy. Alain's
grandfather—also named Gaston—had been a renowned chef in
Paris, running the kitchen at the Grand Hotel. His grandmother
Eleonore had been a chef as well, serving the Baron Rothschild
family at their mansions in Paris and Bordeaux. Eleonore had
been one of the very first female chefs in France.

The elder Gaston had developed breathing problems working

in the hotel kitchen which was located in the basement, with the oven heated with coal and little or no ventilation. The doctor had diagnosed severe lung damage. So they both resigned from their positions and went back to their little native town of Bernay in Normandy and bought an eighty-acre family farm in St Nicolas du Bosc l'Abbe. With his weak lungs, Alain's grandfather could not work the farm, but he managed to become instead mayor of his village for more than two decades. This is where Gaston, the great chef, was born in 1920.

Later in life, Alain would tell anybody who asked that he was *né dans la farine* or "born in flour," a reference to his father's life-long career in baking. It would seem, in young Gaston's life, that his only choice was to become a chef, too. Rural France didn't look much different in the twentieth century than it had in the nineteenth, and sons simply followed their fathers into the family profession. Gaston would follow his father, as Alain would later follow his. Family mattered. Gaston was the patriarch, and, at one point, no fewer than twelve family members were actively involved in the family business, including me!

Living on a farm with chickens, rabbits, pigs, cows, and apples to make cider—or the Calvados brandy for which the Normandy region is famous—was an apprenticeship for young Gaston. His mother was running the farm entirely and was doing the cooking for the employees. Ingredients were transformed into meals all around Gaston, day after day. The practicality of traditional country life was even more preserved by the global depression that was hitting France especially hard. People simply did not have money to buy things, so they produced most meals for themselves from ingredients they could grow. Other things in the village were bartered—a baker would promise to make a *croquembouche* for someone's first communion celebration in return for the block of butter that person brought into the shop's back door.

When he was fourteen, Gaston's parents managed to arrange a three-year baking/pastry apprenticeship for him in Bernay, only five kilometers from the family farm. Paris was always the gold ring, however, as Gaston's own parents knew well from their culinary careers. After winning the title of Best Apprentice of Normandy, Gaston traveled to the capital with his younger brother Marcel and began knocking on the doors of bakeries and famous patisseries, looking for an entry-level job.

Unsuccessful, the two brothers joined the Pastry Guild and went to the headquarters each day waiting for somebody to walk in with a need that aligned with their skill level. On one occasion, they were told there were five-hundred unemployed bakers ahead of them on the list. At night, they tried to make ends meet by unloading trucks at the legendary Les Halles farmers market in the heart of Paris. It was backbreaking work, even for farm boys, accustomed to hard labor. Gaston would later tell Alain about riding his bike around Paris grabbing the backs of public buses to pull him through traffic, sometimes falling asleep as he did so.

In May 1940, the French army was retreating from the Nazi advance; and, while no one knew how long or bloodthirsty the war would be, Normandy eventually seemed like a more peaceful place. So Gaston and Marcel went home. They took to the country roads, already filled with refugees from Belgium and Holland—people with everything they owned on a cart or horse, people who remembered the atrocities during World War I. Everyone was trudging south.

Before World War II, the rural French diet had been fifty percent bread. But all the bakers in Bernay had gone on exodus, and half of the area's population was soon replaced by refugees from the North. With no bakeries and no bread, 8,000 people got very hungry. The city's mayor requisitioned two of the closed bakeries and ordered the LeNôtre brothers to reopen them to feed the masses. And so they did.

As it happened, the woman who became Alain's mother, Colette—a refugee from Paris—was living with her family on the same street that featured Gaston's requisitioned bakery. The two met, took to each other, and were an official couple in almost no time. After that, Colette stood behind the counter exchanging bread for ration tickets.

As soon as Normandy was liberated, but before the war was over, Gaston and Colette mortgaged the farm and bought a bakery in Pont-Audemer, twenty miles from Bernay. The bakery was owned by a certain Monsieur and Madame Tison. The Tisons were known to Gaston because a few years earlier, when he was a mere *commis*, an apprentice, they had fired him. It happened like this: When Monsieur and Madame had returned late to lunch one day, they discovered their young cook had used the six tiny fish he found in the kitchen to feed the six employees. Because no lunch remained for them, they fired the man responsible— young Gaston LeNôtre, the future culinary legend. In a twist of fate, their place in Pont-Audemer became the first foundation of the LeNôtre empire, the world into which Alain and his two younger sisters, Sylvie and Annie, were born.

Alain remembers mostly destruction from his earliest years in the town, placed as it was on the River Risle but no longer featuring the medieval stone bridge that figured in its name. The Germans had destroyed the bridge in their retreat. While many rural American children of the time walked miles to go to school, Alain's experience was quite different, for there was no school left standing in Pont-Audemer. But there was an old woman with a few books on the other side of the river, so each day he walked across the wood-and-cable temporary bridge, which shook and bounced and swayed with every step, to get his first lessons in reading and writing. Dark, steel flower pots filled each house's windows. In a previous life, they'd served as Nazi helmets.

Slowly, with aid from the United States via the Marshall Plan, the town of Pont-Audemer rebuilt. There were, after all, reasons that the place mattered before and would indeed matter again. The town sat upon the main road between Paris and the high-end resort of Deauville and the charming medieval port of Honfleur, so loved by the impressionist painters. Wealthy Parisians, including Marcel Proust, had, for almost a century, been traveling along this road on their way to their villas by the sea. With postwar recovery they started to do so again.

Though it would take Alain years to commit fully to his father's work and world, as a child in Pont-Audemer he would sit on two phone books atop a stool to give him enough height, helping his father knock out tray after tray of a sweet chocolate candy called *palais d'or*. He was charged with carefully placing a square of cellophane atop each hand-dipped chocolate and pressing it gently down with a champagne cork. Later, fresh from the icebox, each piece would lose the cellophane and get a topping of gold. Alain licked his fingers frequently, to get a taste of the rich chocolate that very few in town could afford in those days.

The spartan nature of their living arrangements in a small apartment over the pastry shop led to the first great disruption of Alain's childhood. Though his sisters had a separate sleeping area on the floor above, shared with maids and pastry apprentices, Alain had his only personal space in a tiny "room" reached by crossing his parents' bedroom. This made him more privy than any child would wish to their more amorous moments and, even worse, to their increasingly frequent arguments.

Both Gaston and Colette, Alain came to understand later, indulged in liaisons. As a child, he saw the resulting anger and jealousy, and occasional reconciliation, much too closely. Eventually, the LeNôtres decided, helped along by their nine-year-old son's poor showing in the elementary classrooms, to send him off to the College of Juilly. Originally built as an orphanage for sons of knights killed in the Crusades, it currently served as a boarding school operated by the Oratorian Fathers.

Despite the trauma of leaving home, and in contrast with the life he'd known there, Alain quickly started compiling happy memories. He liked the school and the other boys (mostly sons of large plantation owners in Africa, with exotic stories to share). He liked the priests, their teaching methods, the "tight-ship" schedule of scholastics, sports (swimming even when it was icy outside) and Catholic worship decorum. And he loved the fact that, when his grades were good enough, on weekends he was allowed to take the school bus into Paris to spend time with his aunt and uncle, Suzanne, called Mamie, and André.

Uncle André was a patriot who could have been excused from

military service because a horse accident had damaged his leg.
Instead, he chose to volunteer for the French Army as soon as
the Germans overran Poland in 1939. Only a few weeks into the
Nazi invasion, he was taken prisoner and sent starving to a *stalag*
camp until he was transferred to forced labor on a farm. In all,
Uncle André had spent nearly five years in Germany, becoming
fluent in that language.

From Uncle André, Alain picked up more than enough
German to serve him well·later in life. Once a month, he made
the journey home to Pont-Audemer instead, taking the school
bus into Paris, then the subway, where Uncle André met him to
take him to the train station for the rest of the trip home. It was a
wonderful experience overall, visiting with his parents and developing strong bonds with his younger sisters. When Alain turned
eleven, he made his first communion with his sister Sylvie, parad-
ing after Mass in the main street.

After a decade in their Pont-Audemer shop, Gaston and
Colette finally let their fan club of wealthy Parisians convince
them to sell and move the business to Paris. These Parisians, able
to discern quality French pastry, were among Gaston's first admir-
ers. They made a point of stopping in Pont-Audemer every time
they passed through, enjoying croissant or brioche and a coffee,
and no doubt picking up a treat in a box wrapped in twine to
enjoy later. Colette, Parisian born was the more ambitious of the
couple, and her strong belief in her husband's talents gave the
final push for the move.

The customers promised to come in even more often and purchase even more pastry. In 1957, once the LeNôtre pastry operation had moved to the Rue d'Auteuil in the posh 16th arrondissement of Paris, the patrons made good on their promises. The
street took its name from the village it had once been, which had
the distinction of having housed John Adams for a year in the
eighteenth century when he served as US Minister to France. With
his wife Abigail and their two sons, Adams enjoyed the luxury of a
splendid residence with gardens. Now, the LeNôtres had come to
this renowned area of Paris to seek their fortune.

It wasn't long before Alain entered high school in Paris, known in the French system founded by Napoleon, as the *lycée*. Though he sometimes helped his father in the shop—and still assumed that was his future—he concentrated on his studies. He continued learning German, and he also became passionate about scouting. Some of the weekends, Alain still spent time with his aunt and uncle, who spoiled him with *clafoutis* and *crêpes*. They also had a small black-and-white TV set, where he watched the weekly episode of *Ivanhoe* about romantic knighthood and the cooking show starring Raymond Oliver. The cooking show was a primitive version of one Alain would become involved in years later while apprenticing at Oliver's three-star Michelin restaurant.

When he got drafted for military service in 1964, Alain was deployed to a tank regiment, seen then as the first line of defense, should the Soviets decide to come from the east with intentions on France. Alain learned to pilot both French and American tanks, including "Pattons," sold to the French army by the Americans at the end of World War II. He became a secretary and German translator to his French army captain, first in Trier on the Moselle River (famous for the area's Riesling wines) and finally in the mountain village of Saarburg near Luxembourg.

Army life was pleasant for Alain. His parents had lent him a used Citroën and provided pocket money, so he and his army buddies, when off-duty, could squire their German girlfriends around town. They even shared the rent on a one-bedroom flat in Trier, giving them a place to change out of their uniforms and hit the dancehall in civilian clothes.

Alain fell in love with a blonde "Gretchen"—a *moniker* given any German girlfriend—and once again his language skills proved useful. He also wrote letters in German to a young lady on behalf of a soldier friend, serving as a kind of bilingual Cyrano de Bergerac. He took brigadier training and followed correspondence courses in English and business. Despite all his brushes with romance, by the time of his honorable discharge, Alain had no real girlfriend or interest in a job outside the LeNôtre family business. He returned home to an enterprise that was starting to thrive and that now had twenty employees.

Back in Paris, where Alain earned his apprenticeship diploma in 1961 there was plenty to do around the pastry shop. There was also regular catering to be done, sometimes full savory meals but most often high-end cocktail parties. Alain learned almost every skill he would need within the operation. Then it was time to wrangle, as only Gaston LeNôtre could wrangle, a chance for Alain to cook with the most famous chef in France, then.

Legendary Raymond Oliver was already buying most of his pastries from LeNôtre, serving them to a glittering international clientele at his three-star Michelin restaurant Le Grand Véfour. The establishment dated back to Louis XIII, within the Palais-Royal. Chef Gaston convinced Chef Raymond to accept his son for an unpaid internship. With all his skills, Alain wouldn't be paid a *sous* for working more than fulltime in a hot, airless kitchen. Gaston believed the experience would do the boy good.

In some ways, it did. Alain received an introduction to the real restaurant business, the demanding business of cooking for discerning gourmets, dressed in finery while this unpaid talent sweated and slaved in the basement vault below. Oliver, of course, spent much of his time traveling the world as a culinary ambassador of France, leaving le Grand Véfour in the hands of an excellent head chef.

This chef, however, was only excellent in the morning. He was mostly drunk from wine stashed in his walk-in cooler in the afternoon. A young gifted *saucier sous-chef* filled the void. Alain started out in *garde manger* (cold items like salads, plus the few desserts that weren't brought in from LeNôtre), then graduated to serving as *rôtisseur* (running the broiler) when the previous man stopped showing up. Even though Alain became the *saucier* assistant, he definitely was never taught to be a *saucier* there, to make those iconic French sauces. That knowledge was the *sous chef*'s job security.

Alain only worked directly with Oliver on the 1967 show *Art et Magie de la Cuisine*, taped each week for French television. It was a popular show, though of course no one back then could have anticipated the status of the Food Network and its many siblings, or even of Julia Child, soon to take to the airwaves in America. No, it was simply Alain's job to prep, clean, weight, portion, peel, slice, and chop whatever would be needed to prepare each day's dishes for the camera. And this had to be done in double portions. That prep done, Oliver could concentrate on exchanging witty repartee with the program's lovely host, Catherine Langeais.

For one show, Oliver was about to throw an angry fit thinking Alain had forgotten to prep his *bouquet garni*. Then he realized he'd forgotten to list it, so he sent Alain (with only five minutes until the tape rolled) to dash with a kitchen knife down to the river banks of the Seine to pick what greens he could find on the edge of the water. This was not the least bit sanitary and it was quite a precarious job foraging on the slippery bank; but when this famed French chef added *"bouquet garni"* to his pot, it managed at least to look the part, and the exhilarated staff backstage congratulated Alain for having saved the show.

Alain's *stage* at le Grand Véfour came to an inauspicious end. He was in the middle of service one busy night, pressed into his tiny space, fronting an old-fashioned flat-topped stove and setting a *brochette* of *fruits de mer* under a broiler, when the *sous chef* handed him an empty pot to take to the dishwasher. The seafood needed only less than a minute of that intense heat, and Alain knew he would be fired if he burned it. Needing both hands to carefully remove the *brochette* at the split-second it was ready, he set the dirty pot on the floor against the wall. Seeing this momentary "disobedience" by his unpaid underling, the *sous chef* punched Alain in the chest so hard he dropped unconscious to the floor.

The next day, having successfully avoided being fired for burning the seafood *brochette*, Alain was fired by Raymond Oliver, who obviously had to choose between the *sous chef* and the trainee.

At thirteen, I was elected Miss Agia Paraskevi

CHAPTER 4

And Now You Can Be A Great Actress

An unexamined life is not worth living

PLATO

s Alain learned to navigate the backstage of the glittering world of French cuisine, I dealt with my own shadows. When I turned seventeen, at the time when I was cramming for my final high school exams, my parents went out on the maid's night off. Alone and deeply lonely, I tried to take my own life. Both aspects of that act—the trying and the failing—changed everything. Like the sexual abuse I had experienced at the hands of Sotiropulos, the movie director, it would take years for me to even look directly at the experience.

While pursuing my bachelor's degree in psychology at the University of Houston many years later, I chose to explore adolescent suicide, before I recognized that I was exploring the terrain of my own life. After all, at seventeen I had "everything to live for:" I was enjoying success as a model for the national magazine *Woman* and appearing in ever-larger roles in movies. My parents were supportive, though definitely in that way parents tended to be back then: they never tried to be my best friend.

My father was often away, managing our properties and collecting rent in his spare time. Because he worked at the Bank of Greece headquarters, we always had fresh crisp bills in our house. His horn-rimmed spectacles low on his nose, my father skimmed through the pack before handing it to my mother every month. I heard the whirring sound of the glossy paper, smelled the copper odor and felt that we were quite privileged to have that kind of money. Everyone else's money was dirty and crumbled, and I even resented the old bills I got back from the grocery store.

It was always my mother who was home, and our maid, who certainly did all the hard work. I can only imagine the impact my suicide attempt had on my parents. In some ways, I think now it closed them up to me even more, for fear that something they said would upset me and cause me to try it again. Though the distance in our relationship pained me as a young woman, now, with a mother's understanding, I suppose I should take consolation of their motivation.

It was a strange time. At school, I excelled at some subjects, like French, music and literature, and struggled with others, like chemistry and math. I had eventually made good friends despite my blonde differentness, but even these relationships seemed to change as I became famous. Everybody in the school knew who I was, that my face was on the cover of magazines, that my acting was on display in the movie theaters. Some girls grew jealous and tried to bring me down.

And as for the boys, I feared I would always remain a virgin. My mother's attempt to find a relationship for me was to invite home an older man who practiced medicine in South Africa. He was about thirty and had money, and she told me I should meet him because he was interested in marrying me. The man was attractive, and our encounter was cordial, but when he had left our house I told my mother I wasn't interested in being married to him, whatsoever.

Some of the worst pressures leading up to my suicide attempt had something to do with my final exams, for which I was not prepared, because I was consumed with the modeling business.

I had spent weeks starving myself in order to get as thin as possible. The standard of the times was Brigitte Bardot and her slender figure. I thought mine was pretty plump. And the work was sheer madness, with interminable sittings.

First there was the *couturier* for clothes, and the endless hours trying on dresses one after the other to choose the best for me and the magazine. Then the *coiffeur* for hair—one time my hair had turned to platinum-ash—then the *maquilleur* for makeup where I had to endure all that painting on my face. And then the shooting itself at the farmer's market, the beach, the public squares, under a hot Athenian sun. That job was certainly not for me, but getting a chance to be on the cover of a magazine augmented my chances of becoming a famous actress, and I meant to become one then.

But I suppose the pressure really had more to do with the nature of high school girls and the mean behavior of groups. Some girls spread rumors around the school that the gym teacher was a lesbian. The stories flew that she was making love with some girls and planning to seduce me next. This tale went round and round the school, and considering how little I knew about sex with men, the idea of sex with a woman was even more confusing. Did the teacher I adored really want to do this? I asked myself again and again. Did I encourage it somehow? Might I want it, too? Oh my God. As weeks turned into months, I was haunted by these questions day and night, and my final exams were still ahead of me.

I hadn't planned to kill myself. But when I found myself alone at home that night, I started thinking about this story again, and the more I thought, the more I cried, the more desperate I became. I would never have a normal life, not really. I was bound to be an unhappy movie star, ending up as a drug addict or an alcoholic, I decided, just as I had determined I would never have a boyfriend. I tried to write down my feelings in a notebook, as I would often do throughout my life, but even that release didn't work.

I went into the maid's room, no more than a closet with a small bed in it—and the family's medicine cabinet—locked myself in and cried some more. I opened the cabinet and looked at all the pills the maid kept for dealing with our health issues, and before I could talk myself out of it, I was swallowing one pill after another. I don't know how many pills I forced down my throat, maybe twenty or twenty-five, and I certainly don't know what they all were. I didn't care. When I was finished, I drifted off to sleep, my face soaked with tears.

I woke up in a psychiatric hospital.

There was now much to discuss, and I mainly talked about it with a young, attractive doctor in residence, who came to visit me each day I spent at the hospital. I say young: he was probably only about thirty, but when you picture doctors as being fifty or sixty, thirty seems very young. Though I remember him checking my vital signs and reading my chart, I figured he was a therapist because that's what he did. He asked me questions, gently at first, about what was going on in my life and finally about what was going on that had convinced me to end it. Between the conversations we had and the fact I was wearing one of those flimsy hospital gowns with nothing underneath when he visited, I felt a level of comfort, of intimacy, with the doctor that I'd ever felt with anyone before.

Apparently, the feeling was more mutual than I expected. During the final days before my discharge—before I would move back into my parents' house to start my life again—he told me that he loved me. We were already hugging and even kissing after each session, so I guess it was a natural progression. But honestly, by the time I left the hospital, his gentle questions and encouragements had given me such a feeling of confidence and hope that I wanted to leave the entire experience behind. Including him. That chapter was over for me, and good things seemed to lie ahead. Even so, when I left the hospital, the doctor gave me a gold cross that had belonged to his mother.

"That's for you," he said gently. "Keep it, and don't forget me. I will be waiting for you whenever you feel lonely and want to visit with me."

I did keep the little cross, but I forgot him as soon as I got into my parents' car. I thought I had died, but then I had awakened suddenly with bright sunrays kissing my face, and my nightmares gone. That young doctor who cared about me and said he loved me added to my exhilaration, and a sense of being fully alive dawned on me. Now I did feel I had everything to live for, and I needed to leave the shadows of the past behind.

Because of the time modeling and acting and their aftermath had taken from my education, my grades were not strong enough to go on to college. My dream of becoming a doctor meant I would need to go through ten-plus years of study in medical school; this seemed a hopeless fantasy. Nevertheless, despite my resentment about my mother's lifetime of nudges, I realized that I had established a career in acting. I abhorred modeling, so whatever misgivings I might have about acting, it held the most promise of success. And little by little, the idea of acting—I mean, really acting, on the stage that we Greeks gave to the world—started to appeal to me.

I auditioned for the Drama School run by the Greek National Theater, reciting some of my favorite poems, including C.P. Cavafy. I'd loved his poem "Ithaka," which I did not grasp the meaning of then, but I sensed somewhat the scope and emotion. It seemed to take on fresh meaning for me with each year I spent contemplating my future:

> Keep Ithaka always in your mind.
> Arriving there is what you are destined for.
> But do not hurry the journey at all.
> Better if it lasts for years,
> so you are old by the time you reach the island,
> wealthy with all you have gained on the way,
> not expecting Ithaka to make you rich.

Within a few days, I was told I'd been accepted into the Greek National Theater's three-year professional acting program housed in the theater in downtown Athens. The theater was located in Omoneia Square, the busiest and oldest place in town, where the buildings, cafés and bars were crowded and even dirty, I thought. I would go by bus and spend every afternoon from two o'clock until seven in the evening. Classes were held in the basement of the old theater and my professors were veteran actors in residence. I was thrilled and impressed to be part of the best establishment there was for acting. My journey, into a career and into womanhood, felt as though it had finally begun.

Life at the Drama School took on a welcome routine almost as soon as I arrived. While the only academic class as such was History of Theater and Acting, the courses approached acting from virtually every direction imaginable: drama and comedy, plus helpful physical skills like ballet, gymnastics, and fencing. Stage combat was mostly for the male students, but I was pleased that we got lessons in it, too. Interestingly, while there was much excitement among us about the growing Greek film industry, little or no instruction was devoted to film acting. The presumption was, I understand now, that all real acting was onstage—and that if you mastered that, you could surely get by in movies.

Even as I settled into a schedule of going to classes in the fall and spring—but then going off to make one or two movies during each summer break—many of the troubles that had haunted me in high school followed me. As it had on the movie sets of my earlier life, sex remained a mystery to me. The only book about sex that I had read then was *Lady Chatterley's Lover*, the then-scandalous novel by D.H. Lawrence, but as hard as I tried to find reliable information, nothing explicit came to my attention, and this was sheer frustration. Other girls in my acting program never seemed to miss a chance to talk about men. It was clear to me from their excited conversation that they were not only aware of sex but were engaging in it on a regular basis.

In the end, my lack of experience seemed to undermine my acting. Film after film included kissing scenes; yet, I never felt (or looked) comfortable doing so. And even when a part of me decided it was time to address this problem, it was not as easy as I'd expected.

Drama School did fling me into the center of intriguing

things, all of them involving men. In our circle, there were intellectuals who would spend endless hours remaking the world over coffee or a beer. The side of me that read Dostoyevsky and wrote poetry was attracted to them, but I was more impressed with their intensity than their politics. These guys never seemed to sleep, as long as there was one more societal problem to solve with some socialist program. They could certainly talk.

One night, as people finally were starting to leave the café, one of the men, Alexis, told me he had a car and would be happy to drive me home. And then, on the way, he said it was probably too late for me to go to my house. Why didn't I simply sleep at his place and he would return me to my parents in the morning?

I had always been more naïve than I think I should have been at my age. This time I wasn't naïve.

Life was different after that, but it did not include the man who had ended my sentence of eternal virginity. Instead, I met another young man, Nikos, who had been a child actor in his youth, who saw that I was withdrawn and suffering and who seemed to truly care. Day after day, he took me out for a tea or a lemonade—we were students, and neither one of us had much spending money—and talked with me. I felt so comfortable with him that, sooner than I ever would have guessed, I was telling him of my recent encounter with Alexis. I cried as I told him, whether from sadness or some form of guilt or shame I'll never know. And when I told him the man's name, Nikos completely caught me off guard.

"I knew," he told me. "Alexis was bragging about it."

I have probably never, before or since, felt so humiliated. I cried, and he cried with me. We talked some more, and then cried some more.

"It's not the end of your life," he consoled me. "Now you see, you can cry. Now you have the experience. And now you can be a great actress!"

The summer after my first year of Drama School, I was asked to play a significant role in a film being shot in Chania, on the isle of Crete. I would play the daughter of a rich man, and one of the young male stars of that time would play a guy on the make. In the film, his role was to attempt to sleep with every young woman, and having pretty good luck doing it, not least because he was a handsome young man. This actor, Alkis, looked very sexy to me. Tall, slim and athletic, he had a dark complexion and full lips. His ebony hair fell on his eyes, and he constantly tilted his head backwards to pull it over. When he smiled, his perfectly white teeth made his face shine in an irresistible way. I, who had always had trouble even planting a believable kiss on a man when I was acting, discovered it was possible to have no trouble at all. We kissed and kissed while the cameras were rolling, and we'd barely stop when they weren't. The director and crew would smile and then we'd do the scene again and again. I think they were all enjoying the thrill.

When I look at the cover of the DVD of that movie today, I am struck by how beautiful that young actor was—in some ways, he even seems a bit innocent, which was surely part of his charm to the camera and to all the young women who watched him on the screen. The movie was a huge hit in Greece, and he did seem on the road to major stardom. He also seemed on the road to wherever I was, as he turned up often to declare his undying love for me. But I was honest with him. I told him I did not and could not love him.

While I don't believe it had anything to do with my rejection, that young star, so full of promise at age nineteen, quickly fell from grace, like Icarus after flying too close to the sun. Drinking and drugs played a role, and his movie career crumbled. I saw him years later. On a visit home, my sister Neny hosted a party for me and invited friends from my acting days. The man was there, looking much the worse for wear, and before long he told me that he was still in love with me. Thinking of him, I prefer to recall his unclouded dark eyes that shine out of the cover of that DVD.

In terms of acting, I was progressing. Midway through my three years in Drama School, my experiences in movies and on-stage clicked into focus with all I was learning in class, and I became pretty good. Acting is a craft, after all, and all the talent in the world can't help you much if you don't put in the time to learn. To my surprise, I discovered I had a gift for comedy—at the very moment Greek audiences were grasping at anything to help them escape their memories of world war and civil war. Comedy was just the thing.

Still, I wouldn't want anyone to think my years as an actress were one unbroken triumph. There were roles I went after and didn't get, one in particular. One big-budget film by the standards of that time and place featured international casts working with Greece's own movie star Irene Papas. That would have allowed—or forced—me, accustomed to playing men's daughters, to stand on my own two feet on screen. It's hard to imagine anything more Greek than *Zorba the Greek* and anything more exciting than playing a role in it.

The only role available to me was one of a young prostitute who entertains the colorful Zorba, even if only for a time, during his trips to town. Entertaining men for short periods, of course, still seemed the story of my life, and I was confident I had both the theatrical and life experience to pull it off. The part was not interesting for sure, but the film certainly was, and I was dying to be in a big international film production. The producer, however, just kept looking at me, until he burst out with sarcasm, "You really want to convince me you can play a whore with those eyes?"

"Why not? I am an actress, I can play any role, I know I can," I insisted, perhaps saying more than I wished.

A fellow student of mine at the Drama School got that role since she had played prostitutes already, and Irene Papas got hers, as did Anthony Quinn, and Alan Bates. And, every time I watch *Zorba the Greek* I recall that's how I missed out on seeing myself play the young prostitute.

While I continued to live with my parents after graduating at twenty, I quickly moved into a whirlwind work cycle that seldom allowed me to be home. Free from school, I could make movies twelve months a year—though most movies filmed in Greece still shot outdoors in the summer—and I could also act in theaters at night. During that particular summer, I did both, with the film director picking me up at 6 a.m. to go shoot and bringing me home by 5 p.m. or so. I had to be at the theater at 7:30 p.m., then, do two performances each night of whatever play I was in. Greeks are night owls, so there was always an audience, even for the 10 to midnight show. After graduation, I had a good and long-running role in Kafka's *The Trial.* Not exactly a comedy there.

All this work and performing left me weary, physically and emotionally. There was little time for anything else—for reading, for friends, for making sense of my young life, since obviously this was my life. What it wasn't, it would turn out, was my living, a realization that would eventually end my acting career in Greece.

During one break on a movie set, fellow actors started chatting about how, when and how much they were paid. Getting paid hadn't seemed part of my equation at all. I was living with my parents and had no time to spend any money anyway.

"Yes," one of the older actors assured me. "You just go to the office and ask for your paycheck."

This I did, being very calm and professional about it. I certainly expected to walk away with money, or at least with the promise there would be some if I came back in an hour. Yet, as the older actor looked on, I was told first that the check couldn't be ready until the following week, and then, when I pressed a little harder, that I'd be paid when the movie company felt like paying me. I was shocked, and not exactly consoled when the older actor admitted he hadn't been paid either—even though he had years more experience in the business than I did, and he had a wife and children to support. The more I thought about this situation, the more irritated I got.

We were making hits, films that showed to full theaters all over Greece and sometimes beyond. Somebody was making money from our work. The film company knew we would do this work with no or little pay, either because we loved it or because we had no other options. The picture of this older actor, whose face was familiar in movie houses nationwide, having to beg for his paycheck, and mostly not getting one, infuriated me. That's exploitation of the weakest, I thought. In solidarity with this beloved actor, who could have been my father, I decided to make a point.

The next morning at six, when the director knocked on our door to claim me for another day's shooting, I was still in my nightgown, in fact still in my bed. My mother rushed to my room and pleaded with me to get up and be ready for work, saying the director was waiting in the foyer. I refused. Eventually the director got tired of waiting in the foyer and joined my mother at my bedroom door.

"What's the matter? I am waiting for you!" he said facing me.

"I am not coming," I said.

"And why not?"

'You should be ashamed not to pay your actors, especially the older ones who need the money, that's why.'

'No kidding!'

"I do not want to play in your stupid films anymore," I said.

I had made two films with that company.

He began by pleading, but his pleas turned into threats and finally into obscene screamed insults. "My God, you are crazy. You've lost your mind! What about your career?"

"I don't care!" I screamed back. My mother stood motionless beside the wall, her face pale.

I knew the company would have to replace me, both in the scenes still to be shot and in all the scenes I'd done to this point. It would cost them time, and time would cost them more money, but I didn't care. The director scowled and left me with the Greek version of Hollywood's time-honored "You'll never work in this town again, baby!" In terms of movies, he was nothing if not prophetic.

Some time later, more rested with my days free of movie-making, I was still toiling away with two theater performances of *The Trial* each night. One night, although I felt quite ill, I went to the theater anyway. Once settled into my dressing room, I felt excruciating pains in my stomach area. I was bent over in agony, and I was frightened. Arrangements were made for an understudy to play the role and an ambulance carried me to the hospital, where the diagnosis was peritonitis—a serious inflammation and infection in the appendix. I was lucky enough to get surgery in time, but I did have to remain hospitalized for several days with intravenous fluids and antibiotics. By the time I could make my way back to the theater, I had been permanently replaced.

Free nights joined my free days. There I was, an actress not acting at all. I spent the time dreaming of being someplace else, someplace where cinema was a serious business and the movies were of better quality and scope. The Italy of Fellini and the Cinecittà studios came to mind, along with all those visions of *la dolce vita*. But an effort to learn Italian from a local opera singer came to nothing. Starting a new language from scratch was hard, I found out. My French had always been much better, and France was developing a vibrant film industry, especially with avant-garde directors who considered themselves *Nouvelle Vague*, New Wave. There I could act, I decided; in France I could have real roles.

A chance meeting with my flight-attendant sister's co-worker, a woman who actually had an apartment in Paris, seemed to fling open a dazzling door. So that's it, I decided. Paris it would be.

Gaston and his younger brother Marcel with their parents in Normandy.

CHAPTER 5

Fortune Favors The Bold

> *Life shrinks or expands in proportion to one's courage.*
>
> **ANAÏS NIN**

When Alain returned from his stage at Grand Véfour, the LeNôtre family operated only one pastry shop in Auteuil. Over the next few years, Gaston and Colette expanded to eight boutiques spread west into Paris's chic arrondissements and grew the catering operation into the city's largest and best. That was all made possible in April 1968 by the vision they had to purchase an eight-acre piece of land in Plaisir, a suburb of Paris, with a large kitchen, and then build a professional-caliber cooking school that had not existed in France before. Alain was embarking with his parents on the step-by-step culinary empire building that would someday make LeNôtre a household name throughout the culinary world. First, however, there were the day's croissants to be baked.

Gaston was presiding at the oven station in Auteuil. It was the controlling spot in the operation where all processes from other stations came together. It was also a strategic station where mistakes could not be repaired. The quality of each LeNôtre product depended on skillful handling of this oven station, the largest-at-the-time artisanal four-deck ovens holding twelve steel sheet pans per deck. In order to free himself to be able to focus on the customers, Gaston decided to have his son trained at the oven, keeping the quality extraordinarily high. Alain has talked, as long as I've known him, about how proud he felt when his father asked him to take over the oven.

The oven station was an honor, and Alain excelled at it. It was also hard and technically unforgiving. Moving croissants, macaroons and brioche in, around and out of the LeNôtre oven with the traditional five-meter-long wooden paddle during ten-hour shifts six days a week was draining, especially considering the stress of the split-second timing the process demanded. Alain had to know every inch of the oven, not only that each of the four levels was set at a different temperature but that the back of the oven decks got hotter than the front. Certain items started cooking in the back faster than in front and had to be rotated at the specified time to the front or to a higher level, or vice versa.

It's easy to understand why a master baker like Gaston LeNôtre had kept this oven work to himself for so long. But with his son quickly trained to be in charge, he had the confidence (and the time) to pursue fame and fortune. "I started making money," Gaston told me later, "the day I put down the paddle." With Alain holding the paddle, the business lunged forward, and production space became an issue—it would remain one forever after.

Each spurt of growth created logistical challenges, not only about how to bake enough product but also about how to get it where it needed to be for customers. Techniques were adjusted accordingly—for instance freezing the dough for croissants in one location, then proofing it to allow the dough to rise, and baking in each retail location. That worked technically and also delivered the aromas and freshness of a product baked in ovens on the premises. With even more growth in the LeNôtre family's business, life became one big engineering project, with more trips to look at semi-industrial equipment for purchase, often in Germany. Alain became the designated contractor on each expansion, preparing him for a move no one could foresee at that point.

By the 1975, thanks to his first two dessert cookbooks published with great fanfare by Flammarion, frequent appearances on television and radio shows, paid advertising in every neighborhood newspaper and interviews in national magazines, Gaston LeNôtre was becoming a culinary celebrity. With his baking and catering operations strewn over several locations and branded refrigerated trucks scooting about Paris to make deliveries, Gaston started thinking about consolidation. At this point, savory foods were made in Auteuil but desserts came from his second shop basement in Boulogne, twenty minutes away. He searched for a large location to bring both functions together.

He discovered a large two-story building on eight acres west of the city, once used to supply meals to hospitals. It was located in the still-bucolic cattle and farming countryside of Versailles, in the small town delightfully called Plaisir (yes, meaning pleasure). The future plant was located near an exit of France's very first freeway (known as *autoroute de l' Ouest*). It was larger than anything father or son had dreamed of for their operation, too large by any normal thinking, but Gaston had vision.

Everyone around the company seemed to hate the location, insisting it was too far away and would make Le Notre's image too "industrial." Gaston and Alain disagreed with everyone. They had visited a German baking operation that had sprouted from the rubble of Nazi Germany to six locations in the Dusseldorf area, supplied from a central commissary in Mönchengladbach. They understood that this new facility would permit them to duplicate that German model while still remaining near the gastronomical capital of the world.

As it turned out, not for the first or last time in the LeNôtre saga, the man in charge of auctioning the real estate turned out to be a hunting buddy of Gaston's. As a *notaire*, the man dutifully advertised the public auction, but not too much, just as much as required by law. He then set up a room in his lobby with a table featuring three candles and few chairs in rows out front.

At the advertised hour, the *notaire* auctioneer, received the bid in a sealed envelope from Gaston, lit the three candles—one small, one medium and one large—kept the lobby door open and settled in to wait for the rest of the bidders. For close to half an hour, father, son and auctioneer watched as the small candle burned out, then the medium and then the large. Then the man closed the door, opened the bid and congratulated Gaston on his purchase. The suspense was over. Gaston and Alain were the only people who had shown up.

Alain was placed in charge of readying the huge building to house the main LeNôtre commissary. He and his crews worked around the clock for two months. Taking the place of baking's time-honored rolling pin, the LeNôtres purchased a large modern "dough sheeter" from Germany, becoming the first operation in France to have one. A short time later, with the same scope and scale of vision, the LeNôtres replaced the traditional hand-dipping of candies and other confections in chocolate with a "coating machine" from Switzerland. The plant was now operational.

Gaston was a courageous man and a paternalistic leader who had the right words for each one of his seven hundred employees. I knew that he had lent or given money to his employees who had family needs. And he was always generous, giving lavish gifts of expensive clothing or accessories to his family, and to me. He loved food and desserts, wine and champagne. He loved everything. Whenever we went to restaurants together, he would try each of our plates—to check if the food was good, he said, but really to taste everything his eyes beheld. So all our plates did the rounds to reach Gaston.

When he suddenly got the idea of a new dessert to launch, he would ask, "What are we going to name this one? *Trouvez-moi le bon nom!*" and we had to be creative to find the name that best suited his creation. For instance, Charlotte Cecile—the delectable concoction of fresh ladyfingers, *génoise*, Bavarian cream and chocolate mousse—is named for Alain's daughter Cecile. The beautiful strawberry *Bagatelle* received its name for the rose garden in the Bois de Boulogne. At one point he decided to give a name to the bakery outlets and I was surprised and proud that he accepted my suggestion to call them Boutique, like the fashion luxury stores.

He was a marketing genius, who could turn anything into an opportunity. For example, one year during the week of Christmas, when the LeNôtre boutiques were practically working day and night taking special orders including spiny lobster, caviar, *bûche de Noël* or fancy chocolate boxes, he was even able to turn a stolen truck into a marketing coup.

Here is what happened: All the goods were delivered by LeNôtre refrigerated trucks. One day the driver of one of these trucks was parked on a double row outside the Victor Hugo boutique. Unfortunately he had left the keys in the dash board and the truck was stolen. Before calling the police however, Gaston called all his friends of the major radio stations and advertised a generous reward. The truck full of chocolate boxes had long vanished, but thousands of Parisians who spotted one of the twelve LeNôtre trucks wondered if it was not the very stolen one they should report to get the bounty. It was pure Gaston.

Gaston was not tall, or particularly athletic, but he had charisma and a warm energy emanated from him. His vivid blue eyes sparkled when he talked, and he had learned to keep his naturally charming smile ready for any impromptu photograph. He relished being featured in the magazines and newspapers. It was apparent that Gaston was born to be a star. And he could have been a star in any medium or trade. Alain had great admiration for his father. He was proud to work by his side.

If anybody needed further proof that Gaston was not your typical "French chef," he suddenly decided that he needed to continue his education. He was already a celebrity and was elected President of the Pastry Owners Guild of Paris. His smiling face leapt out from the covers of cookbooks. He ended up writing eight of them with his daughters, Sylvie and Annie, and he saw them translated into five languages. But he knew that in this city, where nobody had recognized his talent back in 1938, there was a market and many opportunities. To him, such things required learning more. Gaston found, to his dismay, that there was no school for professional chef retraining in France, only one in Basel, across the border in Switzerland. He registered under a false name in hopes of not being recognized, a ruse that lasted only minutes into his first day of class.

Everyone at the school was excited to meet this particular "student." The classes were held on weekdays; on weekends, he caught the night train back to Paris for work. It went on this way for a month. When Gaston finished his program, he told Alain "Go there. It will do you a lot of good." However much or little Gaston was gazing into a crystal ball, this commitment to culinary training proved a fateful decision.

Alain's fluency in German meant he could speak easily with the owner of the COBA Basel culinary institute. Alain liked what he experienced there; he was impressed by the hands-on nature of most of the classes and the possibility of asking professional chefs questions while delivered from the production stress he'd experienced in his own frustrating apprenticeship. These were professionals learning from professionals. This school wasn't for tourists, wasn't for wealthy socialites and wasn't for people who simply "loved food." It was for serious people who wanted to improve their chances of success in the incredibly demanding and competitive French culinary field.

The owner took a liking to Alain, especially in light of his father's reputation just across the border. He asked Alain to accompany him by train to a food show in Munich. On the way back to Basel, he started to talk candidly of his situation. He was seventy, he explained, and ready to retire. He had no children to take over the school, so he had decided to shut it down. Besides, he revealed, the Swiss government was about to build a freeway right through where the school stood; this was his opportunity to go spend his golden years at his chalet in the Alps. Alain's excitement was almost uncontrollable. He called his father and, after sharing the news, asked, "Why don't we start a LeNôtre culinary school in Paris?"

Gaston loved the idea. As usual, he told Alain to take care of the project. With his father's blessing, Alain hired Monsieur Ponée, the head instructor chef from the now-closed school in Basel, to teach and run the LeNôtre School in Paris. Six months later, Gilbert Ponée arrived in Plaisir without notice on a day Alain was away. Gaston greeted him warmly and asked him how long he would be in Paris for vacation. The man, as the story goes, turned white and said he had moved his family to Paris for the job Alain had offered him, to run the school. In a flash, Gaston remembered. "Of course, but there is a glitch," said Gaston. "Our building that looked so large one year ago has no space anymore for the school. But don't worry. Alain will build one next to it for you." So Ponée worked besides Alain planning the school.

This first effort at a pastry and catering school went far beyond just being an added amenity for their apprentices. It would be a profit center by itself, and the LeNôtres were proven right. French president Georges Pompidou soon mandated that all French corporations spend one percent of yearly salaries for professional development, and the LeNôtres had what amounted to a monopoly in the culinary field in France. *La chance sourit aux audacieux*, Fortune favors the bold was Gaston's mantra. For instance, once a chef from, say, Avignon in Provence, was re-trained at the LeNôtre school, he returned to Avignon with more tools to create wonderful pastries and be ahead of the competition. The following year, not one but several chefs from Avignon would flock to LeNôtre to play catch-up.

Ecole LeNôtre opened in 1970. Serving hundreds of students a year, the school added even more of a golden glow to the family name. With only two labs and two chef-instructors in the beginning, it would require Alain's expansions two times during its first decade, growing to eight labs and as many instructors.

Once Ecole LeNôtre was up and running successfully, Alain found the time to take a deep breath and survey a landscape that was drastically changed. Rather than a collection of makeshift baking and catering operations, the family had a large commercial central facility on a major route to Paris. That meant the company could bake more, deliver more and, of course, sell more—which meant they could supply more boutiques. Luckily, every class-act landlord in chic Paris was asking for a LeNôtre pastry outlet to grace his building. In short order, the family would build their holdings to ten outlets spread out over the best addresses in Paris, something that no competitor had dared to do. Gaston LeNôtre became undisputedly the Emperor of Pastry and Catering in Paris, which meant France.

The same kind of organic growth that placed Alain's mother in charge of the ten pastry shops put Alain in charge of the catering operation. The LeNôtres had, of course, done catering from the start—mostly high-end weddings and cocktail parties. But there were now requests made for bigger parties, especially corporate events. Alain was asked to move back from Plaisir to Auteuil to transform the former family apartment above the boutique into high-end sale offices. He grappled with the issues of scope and scale and, in two years, grew the LeNôtre catering business from having two fulltime party planners to having six with four secretaries, plus two *maître d*'s to supervise the hundreds of part time waiters.

It was this dramatic expansion that led the family to Pré Catelan—or, in a sense, led Pré Catelan to the family. The refined establishment in the Bois de Boulogne was, by this time, part of a restaurant group with several high-profile operations, including the legendary Fouquet's on the Champs-Élysées. Unfortunately, behind the veil of luxury, the business itself was going bankrupt. It had loans with two banks, both of which were threatening to foreclose. As it turned out, after due diligence, the banks decided they wanted all the real estate the operation held on the Champs-Élysées except the Pré Catelan. They were put off by the nature of the lease. The Belle Époque style ornamental structure originally built as a casino, was the property of the City of Paris, but the tenant was still responsible for virtually every expense to maintain the eighty-year-old building from the cellar to the roof—which was at that time leaking badly.

Pitching Pré Catelan as a venue for catering, a representative from one of the banks approached Alain and asked if the LeNôtres would like to own their own salon, rather than renting space like some *hôtel particulier* all over the city. Alain knew Pré Catelan, and he knew the Bois de Boulogne, and he understood its revered space in the social fabric of Paris. He told the banker yes without any hesitation.

Though the family had many ventures already, Pré Catelan quickly became the most public jewel in its crown. Named after a legendary troubadour, Arnaud de Catalan, from the Catalan province of northern Spain, the restaurant was the latest glittering incarnation on high-value Parisian land that had been a dairy farm as recently as 1900. The success of the renovated restaurant and banquet space was immediate, largely because of the personal charm and sophistication brought to the project by Alain's mother, Colette.

Colette was a lady and a tough boss; all the employees respected her. Elegant and blue eyed, she had the famous Alexander do her streaked blond hair weekly. She wore Lanvin suits and shoes, Leonard shirts, and tied Hermès foulards neatly around her shoulders with a matching brooch. As she had started this business from scratch, she had learned first-hand; and with her intelligence and efficiency, she could turn every catering event into an exquisite affair. She loved luxury and all things refined.

She decorated Pré Catelan using historical detail in the style of the elaborate nineteenth century structure. Glossy decorating and art magazines adorned her office on the first floor, overlooking the restaurant terrace adjacent to the gardens and Bois de Boulogne. It was a sheer pleasure to be a guest among the celebrities at the Pré Catelan and have the chance to dine on fine china with gorgeous flower arrangements and chandeliers, with tuxedoed waiters tending to all your needs in style. Alain cherished that place, for it represented his mother and what she was capable of, and I understand why.

Behind the scenes, there was also a first-rate culinary team under the direction of Gaston's nephew Patrick, who, years later, would become the first instructor at our culinary institute in Houston. During Pré Catelan's first year, Michelin awarded the restaurant its first star; then Michelin awarded the second star during the restaurant's second year.

With the efficiency associated with the best family businesses, the ten retail shops were now handed to Alain Gilles-Naves, who was married to Alain's sister Sylvie. Sylvie was in turn in charge of Public Relations, Marketing and Communications. Younger sister Annie had created a corporate gift department with a sumptuous catalogue. Colette hosted social events, weddings and state diners in Pré Catelan's many salons. Almost every head of a foreign country, president or king paying an official visit to the capital hosted a reception at the restaurant to thank his French hosts. As you might expect, money was no object for such events.

Money was an object, however, to the four armed men who entered Pré Catelan during an annual New Year's Eve gala. They were wearing masks that parodied the French president at the time. But the guns they carried proved they meant business, as they threatened the well-heeled crowd of revelers with what would happen if they didn't turn over all their jewelry, watches, money and other valuables. It was then, faced with the possibility of violence that Colette showed there was one thing she hated and feared more than danger: mistreatment of her guests. She tried, at first, to talk sense into the men.

When they started shooting in every direction, Colette and her assistant Marijo angrily tossed trays of china at the intruders, hitting several in the face. Confused, and not expecting any attack, least of all from the lady of the house, the gang fled into the parking lot, where they were confronted by the restaurant's security guard. They shot and wounded him but, in the process of escaping, managed to drop the only bag of valuables they had collected. Colette returned these to the guests with remarkable calm, and before long the orchestra was playing and the gala started again with the traditional midnight fireworks.

Newspapers covered the attempted armed robbery with enthusiasm, marveling at Colette's grace under pressure and nicknaming her Joan of Arc of the Bois de Boulogne. Only Colette and her dry cleaner knew that her haute couture gown had been pierced by one of the bullets.

During that period, one of Alain's closest female friendships developed with Catherine, a friend of his sister Annie. She was a lovely brunette who hailed from a good family, with a father who engineered tunnels, bridges and harbors for an international French company. Catherine's parents encouraged the idea of a union with the LeNôtres, as every other week, it seemed, Gaston was in the media announcing some new success, and Alain was clearly his chosen heir. The two young people became engaged in July of 1968, with a reception at her parents' garden house, and they were married that October. Alain was very much enamored of pretty Catherine, but she seemed mostly eager to please her parents. The love of the bride and groom was certainly misdirected from the start.

As a model and actress in Athens

CHAPTER 6

Exorcizing The Demon

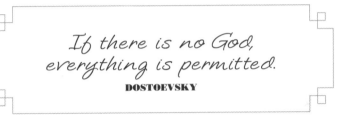

If there is no God,
everything is permitted.
DOSTOEVSKY

W hen you came from a relatively small city like Athens in a country like Greece, Paris in 1965 looked absolutely like the center of the universe. So, of course, I was excited to be there. I knew it wouldn't be easy, since up until then I'd left Greece only for a few days in London. But with my flight attendant sister helping me get a standby seat on Greece's national carrier, Olympic Airways, and her friend telling me I could stay at her apartment for a couple of days, I felt I had all the elements in place for getting my feet on the ground in the City of Light. Everything was happening there—arts, movies, theater, fashion and gastronomy. It was the center of the world.

I rode the Metro to the Place de l'Étoile station and found my way outside through the smelly neon-lighted corridors, finally reaching the sun. Étoile, meaning Star, was the meeting point of twelve large avenues that came together in the form of a star. Constant car traffic swirled on and around the Arc de Triumph. It was the end of May, I had just turned twenty-one, and with my long blond braid, men mistook me for a Gretchen and would follow me throwing words at me in German, of which I understood none but *fräulein*. But their incorrect assumption, and perhaps presumption, did not matter to me as I could walk fast and change directions as I pleased.

I strolled down from Place de l'Étoile to the famous Avenue des Champs-Élysées. The large sidewalks, as wide as the avenue itself, were lined with chestnut trees in bloom and cafés. The *brasseries* were packed with people drinking, eating, smoking, and chatting, the waiters with long white aprons whirled in between the small tables. Some people, by themselves, turned their heads as in a slow-motion tennis match to watch the passersby.

I strolled further down the avenue until I reached the point where the Petit Palais and Grand Palais lay on the right and left side of the boulevard in between gardens. These very richly ornate *Beaux Arts*-style structures with iron and steel framing and glass vaults were built at the same time as the Eiffel Tower for the 1900 Universal Exhibit. Facing the Grand Palais stood the Pavillon Elysée LeNôtre, an elegant palace built at the same time that housed a two-star Michelin restaurant on the first floor and a busy café with terraces and umbrellas for the privileged guests on the ground floor. This was adjacent to the presidential Elysée Palace. I knew nothing about either of these notable locations at that time in my life.

I finally arrived at the magnificent Place de la Concorde with its two monumental fountains, all white and gold with an Egyptian obelisk from Luxor dating from the time of Ramses II in the center. Gazing at all this under a warm May sun, I was filled with awe at the beauty. I could not wait for more. I strolled through Rue du Faubourg Saint-Honoré, bewildered by the luxury of the Hermès boutique, Yves St. Laurent, Carven, Escada, Balmain, Ungaro, Karl Lagerfeld and the store fronts of other sumptuous brands.

I had a growing suspicion now that I was in Paris, that something about my presence in France was amiss. I was perfectly comfortable telling anyone who asked that I was going to Paris to pursue a career in French films. Yet the truth was, I wasn't sure how much I actually wanted to be an actress.

My previous efforts to learn Italian in a week or so had failed, convincing me not to pursue a film career in Italy. Now it was clear that my high school French wasn't even close to being good enough in Paris either. I would do what I could to find movie work in Paris, even arranging a face-to-face meeting with Greek-born *émigré* director Costa Gravas, of the famous movie *Z* who only confirmed how difficult it would surely be for a foreign actress, like me, who barely spoke French. My head wasn't in it anyway. In those first days and weeks, as I realized my heart wasn't in the movies, it became clear that my heart wasn't in anything.

My sister's friend was true to her word about the apartment, though she stressed she had a boyfriend and I couldn't stay more than a couple nights. Those couple of nights, coupled with my walking the boulevards of Paris every waking hour, led me to the University of Paris. It was end of May, and classes had just let out. The school allowed me to rent a room in one of its dorms—nothing fancy, just a studio apartment with a bed and kitchen and a bathroom down the hall. But it was a place to sleep.

Sleeping was all I did there anyway. I was amazed, enthralled, captivated by my long walks along the Seine, past Notre Dame, around the Étoile and across Concorde, soaking in all of the fancy shops and crowded luxury cafés. I loved watching the people strolling the Champs-Élysées—I was sure I would encounter a celebrity soon—and all this suited me just fine. So I strolled and strolled, streets and avenues, my head up, hands in my pockets, no strings attached. I felt free. I felt clean. I felt new.

I had an address—you know, a friend of a friend kind of thing—that a classmate at the Drama School had given me. This young woman worked at American Express in Paris and would, I thought, be a possible friend in a city full of strangers. I went to see her at her office in rue Scribe, and we agreed to meet for dinner. I didn't want to jump to conclusions, but having dinner with friends in Paris seemed like a step in the right direction, and she was bringing her boyfriend to dinner. It was not lost on me, with nobody in my life, that everybody I tried to do things with in Paris had a boyfriend. I wondered if all the boyfriends were already taken.

We met for dinner, and she was very Parisian looking, slim and self-assured with chestnut hair touching her shoulders. Her boyfriend seemed nice too—tall, slender, green-eyed and fair-headed, as well as quite funny, I couldn't help noticing. But they were together. So I was surprised—very surprised—that as the three of us sat at that table eating and drinking wine, the boy-friend started nudging against my leg. His girlfriend didn't seem to notice, so he was clearly accomplished at such blatant flirt-ing. This flirting continued a day or two later, when he somehow came up with my phone number, certainly not from me, and called to ask me out for a date.

"How come?" I asked the young man, whose name was Alain Casau—(there were lots of Alains in Paris at that time). "You have a girlfriend, don't you? You know, the woman who introduced me to you at dinner!"

"Oh her," Alain said. "She isn't any big deal. She doesn't care about me. She wants to go to America and marry a millionaire. So why should I care, either?" He seemed so sincere.

We went out on a date, and I realized I couldn't possibly face the young woman again. I hope she finds her American million-aire, I thought. Alain Casau was charming, and having heard of my movie plans, he asserted he was involved in the film industry somehow. Although I believed him at the time, that proved to be less than true. He did own a camera, but he certainly wasn't making films.

Instead, he loved reading science magazines and had a pas-sion for science fiction. He loved to gaze up at the stars, and we began going out to look at them together night after night. He always pointed out moving lights he believed were UFOs. UFOs were a big thing to Alain; he read books and magazines about them all the time, which no doubt helped him see them in the sky. He was twenty-two, and I was twenty-one, and before too many star-gazing sessions I was in love in the City of Love.

Alain Casau owned a Renault Gordini, for which he had built a second motor so it could blast around like a sports car. Together, we explored every delight the city and its surrounding country-side had to offer. We even paid visits to his adorable grandmother, which made the relationship feel even more official, even more real. He was actually living in her apartment, saving money for girls and motorcycles, I suppose. I also met his mother, Jacqueline, a charming, pretty woman, remarried to an engineer who worked for Jacques Cousteau, so she was busy travelling with him and Cousteau a great deal for their diving expeditions and not overly involved in tending to her son. But from the very first moment I met her, I had the impression that she liked me.

Throughout the summer, I was still staying in the dorm when I wasn't going about with Alain Casau. I knew that my time there would come to an end as soon as the students returned for the fall. I spotted an ad in the paper offering a room rent-free for only the cost of phone and electricity. In return, the tenant would stay with the man's nineteen-year-old daughter, especially while he traveled on business to places like Africa. The apartment was not in a great neighborhood, but the financial arrangement was too good to pass up. Before long, I was living at that apartment, working as *fille au pair* for my pocket money, and taking French classes at the Alliance Française. And, of course, dating Alain with an eye on getting married to him.

Marriage had become the only plan I had left. My family was far away and close friends were nonexistent. As beautiful as Paris was to me, I was living in a city where I still spoke only the begin-nings of the language. I had no real job, no meaningful activities, and in so many ways no life. So I proposed. You know how men are: you have to tell them what they want. But Alain Casau was adamant about not being interested.

"This would not be possible," he said earnestly "I'll never be faithful. I just can't. It might be genetic."

"That was the past, and it's over. Now you will be," I said. I earnestly believed it. "Because now you're in love with me." As he was not responding to the last, I added, "If you don't, I'm leaving you."

When he didn't say anything, I was devastated. Completely lost, I packed up my one suitcase and moved back to Athens, back to my parents' house. I had no dreams left. Again, I cried a lot. My parents could do nothing to help me. I had failed in Paris, failed at getting married every bit as much as I'd failed to have a meaningful career in the theater and movies. My poetry had gone nowhere either, as much as I loved writing poems. Perhaps I had no talent at all, I pondered. Alain and I kept talking on the phone almost every day. He was sweet and tender, and I was dying to be with him again. I had left him in the beginning of the Christmas season. By the end of January he decided he wanted to see me and he could not live without me. He asked me to come back to Paris and marry him, if that would make me happy.

We were married in a Greek Orthodox church in March. Alain went along with the ceremony although he didn't believe in religion. Even I was out of faith then, essentially out of everything. My parents and my sister Neny flew to Paris to see me wed in a Jean Dessès dress I picked out alone.

After the wedding reception at the Pavillon des Princes, Alain and I drove the Renault Gordini to the Côte d'Azur for our honeymoon. We spent time in Nice, with all its grand old hotels along the waterfront, la Promenade des Anglais, then Villefranche and Menton and finally we made it over to Monte Carlo. That was special to me, as so many famous Greeks, from opera diva Maria Callas to shipping magnate Aristotle Onassis, were associated with the place. I felt like I was home. After that, however, our love week was up and we had to start a new life.

With jobs as with women, Alain Casau got bored easily. He had been working as a manager for LaFarge, a building material company, but shortly into our marriage he left to join his half-brother selling motorcycles. For that we had to borrow 10,000 francs from his father, who was making lots of money in real estate and the stock market, with the promise to reimburse him six months later. Although motorcycles were a hot new thing in Paris at the time, in six months we had not made enough to reimburse him, yet.

Eventually, though, the motor shop became a money machine. We didn't have a plan, exactly, but we knew there'd be
something, a logical next step for us as a couple. I had gotten a
job at the office of Olympic Airways in the reservations department, having perfected my English and French. In those days,
before computers, it was a busy place booking, changing and
cancelling air tickets.

One time we had to cancel and re-route every passenger on a
flight from New York to Paris. Onassis was taking over the plane
to bring his fiancée Jacqueline Kennedy and his court to his
newly bought island, Scorpios, in the Ionian Sea close to Ithaca,
for the wedding. Often times we had celebrities, like Charles
Aznavour, buying an economy ticket and calling for an upgrade
to first class—but of course!

As the world's most famous Greek in his day, Onassis seemed
to be everywhere. He owned the building our offices were in, and
he was in and out regularly. I rode the tiny two person elevator
with him once, just him and me, so close, and he made a point of
flirting with me a little. Being a Greek man, how could he not?

"Hi!" I said, "I work for you here on the second floor!"

He smiled at me and retorted charmingly, "I wish I worked for
you, mademoiselle!" We said *au revoir* to each other as the elevator reached the ground level.

Onassis was short and half bald with bulging big eyes. Probably
his most interesting habit, though, was flying baguettes from Paris
to Athens on one of our daily flights. I'm not sure how much he
paid for that, but he really loved his French baguettes.

After a couple of years of a no-problem marriage, making
love, eating out, going to country inns for the week-ends and
hiking around, my mother started pestering,

"Why are you not having a baby yet?" She would ask, "What
is the matter with you? Go and see a doctor, at once. That is not
normal."

Well, I felt normal, yet I had never thought of having a baby.
I was working, travelling, reading. Essentially my life was quite
simple. I went to a special doctor just to please my mother. There

was something wrong with me, it turned out, and that was quickly fixed. I soon got pregnant with my first daughter, Nathalie. And within a short time after her birth, I was pregnant again with my second daughter, Armelle. I had to relinquish my job at Olympic as the airline did not provide extensive maternity leave at that time.

One day when I was eight months pregnant and home alone, Alain's father stopped by to visit.

"You'd better keep an eye on your husband!" He warned.

"What do you mean," I said, frowning.

"Well, I don't know…are you still making love together? You are a couple, right?"

I got embarrassed by such a question coming from a man with whom my husband and I only had formal dinner with once every two months at his opulent 16 *arrondissement* apartment. His second wife initiated the dinner, to be proper, doing her BA, *bonne action*. That was not the kind of conversation I would ever expect from this father-in-law, whose only dinner conversation consisted of the stock market and his success there.

As I was speechless, he continued, "With my wife, we'd make love all the time, you bet, everywhere, in the bathtub, on the floor, on the balcony, that's what you are supposed to do as a young couple."

He was pacing the wood floor of our living room, stylishly, very assured, his tailored blue suit fitting him perfectly, his lightly gray hair glued on the sides. Abruptly changing the subject, he tossed out, "I suppose you don't have my money yet? The six months are overdue, you know?" Then suddenly he changed tacks again, "There are some nice pieces of furniture here, I can see."

"We're getting by," I retorted. "The store is doing very well, and we'll get the money to you soon."

"Business is business," he snapped. "This magnificent *armoire normande* here, for instance, I bet it is worth ten thousand. I am certain—ask an appraiser—then we don't have to talk about this anymore." He smiled big, making sure I got his message. "Right," I said bemused, "You are right. I'll talk to Alain tonight."

He left my apartment, his sardonic smile still on his face. My thoughts went to Alain. No, we certainly did not make love as much as usual lately. But that was due to my pregnancy, I supposed, maybe to the routine, and his keeping long hours away from home. When I confronted him later in the evening about his father's visit, he concentrated on the idea of immediately selling the *armoire normande* that his grandmother had given us as a wedding gift if it was worth that much.

"And you know something?" he added. "We'll make tons of money, soon, I promise. I'll make it up to you, and we'll leave this city. I'm sick of it. We'll go far in the country, where we can breathe fresh air and live like decent human beings, not like we do here in Paris with its dirty crowd. Here, even my half-brother would screw me if he had the chance." This turn of events made me sad about our relationship with Alain's father, but it did not bother Alain. He was used to this. His father had taken him on a vacation trip only once in his lifetime, to a ski resort, and he had reminded him year after year that he should have been grateful.

The truth is Alain was never a lover of Paris, or art, or social events, or travel. Alain Casau found solace in science and science fiction, and smoking. Smoking was his escape. He always avoided any intimate conversation with me on the subject. He never complained, got violent, or became angry. He had made his peace with his past and family. Now he convinced me that a country life would be better for us both. I had no choice then but to believe that, indeed, a life in the country, away from Paris, would suit us better.

What I did not know then was that he was having an affair with his half-brother's girlfriend. I could not imagine that then. I continued to love him and trust him. He was my husband after all.

I had been stashing money away at the bank to build us a house. And by then I was looking at all kinds of architects' plans for my dream house. I had designed it, complete with a fireplace and outdoor grill, round windows and French doors, my bath, his shower, the kids' room, the guest room, and a fancy kitchen. I also designed the garden, choosing the trees and flowers of the Pyrenees region, because that was where we were going. As soon as we had enough money, Alain and I left Paris for a small town near Pau in the southwest of France, a place called Tarbes, where I built my dream home.

Compared to the go-get-them life of Paris, Tarbes was easygoing. Many people worked in the morning and skied in the afternoon, or played tennis each day. From our terrace, we could see the peaks of the Pyrenees, snow clad year round, and our yard was so big that neighbors were out of sight. We had dogs—I accepted that. And we spent our Sunday afternoons reading in front of the fireplace. School and daycare were not far from home for our daughters; and it wasn't long before I was playing tennis all the time, too. Being competitive, I always played to win, and in short order I was champion of the Pyrenees. I accomplished this by learning how to be patient. I didn't play spectacular tennis, or beautiful tennis, but I understood how to hit the ball across the net as many times as possible. I played to win, even if I had severe cramps or blistered fingers.

I could say I was happy at this point, but based on what I would come to understand later, that would be too strong a statement. My life was organized and running smoothly. We had friends to ski with, dine and drink with, and Alain had cousins living close by who were a big help with the children.

Alain Casau worked very hard in his new business and I helped of course. We opened a *tabac*, that strange little French shop that sells cigarettes, stamps and newspapers with an attached bookstore and a gift shop. I liked working in the bookstore, since each day brought a new shipment of books. I was always reading something interesting to me, so the days passed and went. And since the lot across the street was empty, Alain and his cousin opened a dealership selling motor homes and RVs, which were just taking off as a revitalized postwar French economy rediscovered leisure. They even opened a dating and matchmaking agency a few miles away and spent most evenings there.

I did not pay attention to these enterprises, since in addition to tennis, another new activity had entered my life—painting. It had started in Paris. I loved going to all the museums and especially the Jeu de Paume on the place de la Concorde, and while pregnant with my second daughter, I craved vivid colors. I particularly embraced Impressionist paintings. Cezanne became one of my big influences for still life, centered around fruit on tables, though I had no talent for recreating his incredible landscapes. I also loved the human element, painting portraits of my girls and myself, even of Alain, who sat for me while I painted what might have been my best picture of all, and my last one. There he was, youthful and slender and handsome. And there he would remain in my mind forever.

Alain Casau had been right. He didn't believe he could be faithful to me, and he wasn't. I was naïve again. When he told me he had to work late, I believed he was working, not spending intimate hours with his other woman. A friend finally told me the truth. Alain didn't deny it, of course, since he could eternally have the excuse that he'd told me so. I could have chosen to live with it, as many French did for generations, but I was not French. I packed up my bags once again, and this time, my daughters' bags as well, and drove the three of us to the only place I knew to turn, my parents' house in Athens. I hoped to reflect and regroup and find family support.

Instead, seeing me alone with my two girls, my mother showed no mercy or joy, and my father took it especially hard. He had no place in his traditional world view for divorce. He even brought in a priest to exorcize the demon inside me that obviously was causing all this trouble. The priest sprinkled the house with holy water, then my family, then me and the girls. My father was relieved, believing in this kind of therapy and exorcism that people were using in Crete. I didn't believe this myself, but the fact that my father believed it and was relaxed afterwards took some burden off me. In any case, my mother retorted, there was no life for me as a divorcee with two kids in Greece. I had to go back to France, she said, where men are braver, more modern and, ultimately, a good deal wealthier.

I talked to Alain on the phone, again and again, but it was clear he had no intention of changing his ways. Although he would not say anything about separating or divorcing—he did not want to hurt me, certainly, or take responsibility for his actions, I suppose. But for me, I just could not stand knowing that my husband was in love with another woman. Now I had no life in France or in Greece, I thought. I had no friends anywhere who didn't belong to my dying marriage—those skiing, tennis, business, or socializing friends. That world would all go away, I knew. Still, in order to get a divorce from Alain Casau, I packed my daughters into the car once again. I drove us across Greece and Italy, stopping only for gas (I was afraid of pickpockets, or since we were a car full of females, of much worse) and finally reached Tarbes, after spending the night at Aix en Provence, in the company of my mother-in-law, Jacqueline, who lived there because she liked the sun and the sea.

A lawyer I consulted when I reached Tarbes said I could not get a divorce, that leaving Alain Casau would not be advantageous. "Yes, I can. And yes, I will," was my reply.

In the weeks that followed, I got a divorce, sold our house for a profit, used that money to buy a flat near the Opera in Paris, sent my furniture to Paris, enrolled the girls in school nearby, got a daytime job in a travel agency and set up housekeeping in the ashes of my life. Fortunately I had a Greek friend there, Jenny Roucher, who had worked with me at Olympic Airways. She helped me lovingly and generously, housing my family before I moved to my Opera flat. She was working on her Ph.D. in Linguistics at la Sorbonne, so we spent time musing and chatting together about the origins of language.

"You know," Jenny consoled me, "You are hurt in your ego, because he cheated on you. But think about it. You had nothing in common, intellectually, spiritually, or otherwise. You had even never travelled together!"

I thought about it for a few moments, "You're right," I said, realizing the truth in her words. "My feelings are hurt, but I am not. Our marriage was not fulfilling."

I saw Alain's father again during this time. Once more, he arrived offering unsolicited commentary on my life. Before I said anything, he warned me that I should not expect any money from him whatsoever. As for his granddaughters, he said he'd never met them and did not care about them.

"I hope you can manage," he added, glancing at my nicely decorated living room. "Rest assured," I told him. "I have a job and enough money to go around, for my two daughters and me."

One of the few bright spots at this time was my former mother-in law, Jacqueline. As I had sensed from the beginning of my relationship with Alain, she liked me. We used to play scrabble together in French and I often won. She admired me for that because my native tongue was Greek. She was a woman with many passions, like me I suppose. She had dared to divorce her first husband, Alain's father, and venture to another marriage, and a new life. And now I discovered she knew all about her son.

"You were too good for him anyway," she said. "He was not worthy of you."

I didn't want to listen to such talk; I didn't want to listen to anything. But she kept talking.

"You know," she told me, "don't be sad or disappointed that you divorced my son. You deserve to be treated better. I am serious—there are other men out there."

"Ok, right," I said. "So what, what am I supposed to do?"

"Do what I did."

"And what was that?"

"Place an ad at *Le Chasseur Français*," she said.

Le Chasseur Français was an old and classy magazine addressing gentlemen farmers. It included a matrimonial ad section in the back-pages. It's worth pointing out, in today's age of online dating websites, that no one I knew in Paris in 1980 would admit to advertising for a mate in a magazine. When I finally gave in and wrote the ad, I used most of the words my mother-in-law had given me. But it needed my own truth, I felt. That would make it clear for once and for all who I was, what I was so hungry for, and how painful it was to be at the center of the world, in the City of Light, and feel like I was drowning.

"S.O.S," I wrote across the top of the ad.

Alain as catering manager at LeNôtre
France in 1979

CHAPTER 7

Living Like Gods In France

Life started out comfortably enough for newly-weds Alain LeNôtre and wife Catherine. They lived first in an apartment near Versailles and then, when Alain was asked to take over the LeNôtre catering operation, they moved into a chic neighborhood called Passy, conveniently close to Auteuil. In the beginning, as their children, Cecile first, then Charles, were born, Catherine stayed home to care for them. A bit later she was hired by Gaston and Co. to manage the flagship boutique in Auteuil. She also helped to open each new LeNôtre retail store by training their staff. She handled her duties very well, a fact not lost upon family members concerned about the retail side now that Alain's mother, Colette, had left the Auteuil boutique and had become the undisputed queen of Pré Catelan.

Alain LeNôtre's new role was in sales, marketing, management and logistics. His mandate was to increase revenues, and that meant selling new things to old customers and finding new customers. The great Gaston was the company's PR machine, always on TV and in the glossy magazines, but it was up to Alain to turn such general good feeling about the LeNôtre brand into signatures on catering contracts and deposit checks in the bank account.

One of his first innovations was sharing sales leads with the luxury silverware brand Christofle, a fixture at baptisms, first communions, engagements, weddings and other high-profile events enjoyed by France's rich and famous. In those "primitive" days before the Internet, Alain determined that anyone able to afford Christofle was able to afford LeNôtre, and of course vice versa. When the company had an event, or even several in a single day, he knew exactly what to send in which truck, what equipment needed to be rented and which staff or temps needed to be sent. There was no customer to be found, his thinking went, that couldn't be impressed with the LeNôtre's excellent food, service, and creativity.

From 1970 to 1975, Alain and Gaston led the charge to capture the catering of everybody who mattered in France. There were standing contracts to handle parties for the French foreign office, the prime minister of France, as well as parties staged with luxurious abundance in landmarks like the Presidential Elysée Palace and many Chateaux, even Versailles. There were also lasting relationships with the likes of Dassault, Cartier, Christian Dior, Hermès, Moët et Chandon, Total, Mercedes and Ford France.

While Pré Catelan did not achieve higher than two-stars from the revered Michelin guide (three star is the maximum in the Michelin scale), Gaston proved the leader of a crowd of ten regional famous chefs who had three stars (out of a total of twenty-two chefs in France). Rather than sit up nights worrying about this, he organized his friends into a loose-fitting confederation to merchandise the act of being a famous chef itself. Well-heeled clients could order an event featuring, say, LeNôtre, Bocuse and Vergé (a trio that would emerge within this larger group), and the group could organize the affair. And at the end of the day, who better to organize anything than Alain?

The most challenging event of this type, featuring eight of the most famous French chefs, each staging his own signature buffet, was for 800 members celebrating the 500th birthday of the most affluent country club in Portugal, Gremio Literario. Alain was sent over early to scope out the setting in a castle overlooking the Tage River. The situation was challenging because of the lack of kitchen space. The good news was that the *palacio* had a large fencing room, a kind of ancient dueling academy in a long *orangerie*. Alain convinced the customer to do the hard work of bringing in gas, water and electricity so the chefs could operate the stoves—which Alain had to rent, have delivered and installed as well. It was a huge undertaking but, as it turned out, the client had bottomless pockets.

As the big day arrived in Portugal, Alain was already at the venue and Gaston had shipped twenty-five Styrofoam containers for his dessert buffet, as he had decided not to make the pastries in the fencing room. When Gaston was in his Citroën-Maserati for the trip to the airport, Alain phoned him, saying that Chef Troisgros needed hay for cooking a *jambon au foin*, an old recipe for a whole ham slow-cooked with hay. It must have been quite a vision: the famous Gaston LeNôtre in his luxury automobile, pulling off the road to steal hay from a farm. The Portuguese customs went smoothly, four cases of beer doing the trick. The officer apologized, saying he still had to open one of the twenty-five containers. He chose one at random and, sure enough, he picked the one with the hay!

This was the 1970s, what many might call the Golden Age of Franchising—in America this involved the fast-food industry, of course, but as a business model it quickly moved through virtually every type and level of enterprise. It did not take the LeNôtres long to see franchising as a way to take on partners in growing their business without going too far out on a financial limb.

Alain was asked to hurriedly pass the catering management to his brother-in-law Alain Gille-Naves (a friend from his scouting days) and move back to Plaisir to start a full franchise department.

By then, LeNôtre had received a request to handle a three-week-long French food and wine festival at an upscale Berlin department store called Kauf Haus Des Westen (KDW) owned by the Hertie group. Berlin at that time was an island of freedom and abundance behind the Iron Curtain, located within, but not part of, communist East Germany. The KDW store was roughly equivalent to Bloomingdale's in New York but more diversified. Its customers loved the promotion with the LeNôtres—the store advertised the big event as "Living Like Gods in France."

KDW suggested some kind of ongoing partnership. The two sides struck a permanent franchise deal. The LeNôtre line was now manufactured at KDW with the exception of the LeNôtre chocolate candies and the LeNôtre fine groceries. The family's line of wine and champagne was supplied from France, as well as all the packaging. Alain decided to create an export department in Plaisir for the German (and later the Japanese) franchisees. Eventually other stores in Hamburg, Munich, and Stuttgart were added. Not only would the LeNôtres support and keep an eye on these outlets, but Alain would bring many KDW German chefs to the Ecole LeNôtre in Plaisir for training. But of course!

In a world created with aid from the postwar Marshall Plan, a reborn Japan came next. The family was approached by Seibu, a conglomerate of Japanese businesses, railroads, departments stores, stadiums, restaurant chains etc. They had observed the KDW-LeNôtre success in Berlin and were eager to hang the LeNôtre shingle on a series of retail pastry-bakery cafés, extremely upscale places that would feature waiters in tuxedos. The initial territory covered half of the island nation, the other half being added in later years. In all, the family helped open fourteen franchised shops in Japan. For their part, the Japanese (like the Germans) proved loyal professional franchisees, always following the LeNôtre standards to the letter.

Brazil's economy was doing well in the 1970s. One wealthy Brazilian was building the Rio Palace Hotel at the junction of Ipanema and the Copacabana beaches. He was advised by the undisputed king of Parisian nightlife, Jean Castel, to get technical assistance from Bocuse, Verge, and LeNôtre. But the negotiations dragged out so long that, by the time the deal was done, Bocuse and Verge had dropped out to pursue other opportunities in Brazil. The franchise belonged to LeNôtre alone.

Castel planned to duplicate his very exclusive Parisian nightclub in the Rio Palace basement. Gaston sent Alain and a group of their best French chefs and a *maître d'* to create a fancy restaurant to be named Pré Catelan. In addition to the restaurant, they had to plan the banquet department, room service, tea room, wine cellar, and everything else. Gaston and this franchisee became such good friends that, at the end of the five-year contract, Gaston allowed the Rio Palace hotel to continue the use of the Pré Catelan name for its fine-dining restaurant.

In the mid-1970s, with LeNôtre operations springing up with such frequency around the world, it was only a matter of time before the Saudis and then the Kuwaitis wanted to get involved. Alain hired a Lebanese engineer from Paris as translator/advisor following an invitation to exploratory meetings in Jeddah and later in Kuwait. He felt he should be cautious. Beirut was very much on Alain LeNôtre's itinerary too, since they had a distributor of LeNôtre chocolates there who wanted to become a franchisee.

Unable to meet with his potential partner, who was in the hospital, shot by a Palestinian in the civil war, Alain discovered his shop in the Christian quarter. It was protected with sandbags almost to the ceiling, since the shop had been burned to the ground during Syrian/Palestinian attacks a few days before. Alain agreed to let his translator take him home during a truce to visit his Christian village close to the mountains.

The village was circled almost completely by a high cliff topped with minarets and (this being Lebanon in 1975) mortars that rained down shells on them. The villagers were heroic. They raised enough money among themselves to buy their own mortars and dug trenches from which they could defend themselves from nighttime commando raids. Alain was more than a little relieved when he retrieved his passport in the Beirut airport and made a safe exit with his translator from the devastated metropolis, back to the City of Light.

By the late 1970s, Alain LeNôtre had served his father very well. He had become the family's operations genius, the one automatically expected to step in whenever Gaston dreamed up some crazy new money-making scheme. There would be no LeNôtre empire without Gaston and Colette, naturally. But at this point in the family's history, there would also be no LeNôtre empire without Alain's gift for organization. He had every reason to feel proud of his contribution. He was elected deputy general manager and convinced the family to start a 20% profit-sharing system for all 700 company employees, with managers and key chefs to receive a total of 11% of company stock.

Yet, sadly, Alain was about to have his entire universe yanked out from under him. He slowly began to suspect his wife was having an affair.

There was one huge difference between Alain LeNôtre and the typical French male, whom he resembled in so many other ways. Even after World War II and the French culture's on-again, off-again embrace of anti-clerical, leftist existentialism, Alain remained fervent in his Catholic faith. So, even as his father's missions kept him away from his family for long days and sometimes nights, Alain absolutely resisted the temptations of infidelity. He often told me that he had missed his children growing up. In his mind and heart, there was no other way to be a husband and father, or even to be a man—ignoring the evidence all around him that many did not live by the same rules. His courage and faith in God, and in others, were the first things I would love about him.

Yet suddenly, the intimacy in his marriage to Catherine had dried up, gone away. The other man—Alain still called him his "rival" when we became close enough to talk about this, with a dash of chivalry the situation did not deserve—was none other than a young, handsome, ever-womanizing LeNôtre chef, someone Gaston and Colette had generously taken under their wings. Alain considered this man a friend, as well.

The man was talented enough as a chef, of course. To survive with the LeNôtres, one had to be. But there had always been

ACTRESS & MODEL

◄ *On stage in 1964 in Kafka's* **The Trial.**

▼ *Modeling and acting in Athens.*

ΧΡΙΣΤΟΥΓΕΝΝΑ

ΚΟΥΖΙΝΑ!...

ΓΥΝΑΙΚΑ

FAMILY

▲ Alain in Normandy at age four.

▲ Robert Mondavi and Marie prepare for the hunt at les Bastes, Sologne. Alain's sister Annie with her first husband are behind.

▼ Alain, during his military service in Germany.

▲ Wedding cake, as only a LeNôtre could create.

▼ With Alain and Gaston at the opening of LeNôtre Paris in Dallas' North Park Mall, December 1983.

▲ In my silk wedding dress by Parisian couturier Angelo Tarlazzi at our wedding reception.

With all our children. Cecile, the eldest, holds newborn Gaston Jr.

A LeNôtre family reunion at our Hedwig Village home on the occasion of Gaston Jr.'s first communion

Gaston celebrates Gaston Jr.'s birthday in the villa in Cap Benat, France; the LeNôtre Chef jacket is in the background.

Alain and Gaston in full hunting gear in Sologne.

Our five grown-up kids sitting, Charles, Cecile, Nathalie, Armelle, Gaston.

With Nathalie in the middle and Armelle, my daughters.

Gaston LeNôtre and Colette pose for a Paris Match six-page spread with me and Alain, his sisters Sylvie and Annie and their children, 1981.

SCHOOL

▼ *Students outside of the School celebrating after Graduation.*

▲ *Alain puts the last touches on a wedding cake.*

▸ *Student buffet prepping.*

▶ Chef Kris and students in the School's vegetable garden.

▶ Student pastillage center pieces.

2014 GALA

▸ *With Ernie Manouse, PBS Anchor/Producer at the 2014 Champagne et Chocolat Scholarship Gala.*

▲ *With Margaret Alkek Williams 2014 Gala Honorary Chair, and Jane Page Crump, 2014 Honoree.*

MEDAL

◄ Chef Daniel
Boulud, just after
presenting me with
the medal.

▲ With Chef Thomas Keller.

▼ With Chefs Daniel Boulud, Thomas Keller, Jerome Bocuse, Alain and the staff of Kris Bistro during the ceremony in which I received the French Medal of National Merit.

jokes about him around the kitchens, to the delight of Gaston, about his Don Juan escapades, about how he kept mistresses all over Paris, and about how they even did his laundry between visits, giving him an excuse to always go back. Alain was understandably slow to believe what he heard among the whispers: that one of this man's mistresses was his own wife.

In my opinion, the beginning of the end came when the LeNôtres—still oblivious or at least unconcerned—started treating the young chef as an adopted son. By this point, Alain had acquired a sailboat in Lisbon, Portugal—he always loved life on the water—and invited Catherine to sail with him around Spain back home to France. She joined him only as far as the Baleares, then insisted on flying back to Paris, back to her lover. Once Alain got back in Paris, he confronted Catherine with the affair and she finally admitted the truth. Alain forgave her, as she said that the relationship was already over. Alain later got proof that was not true. No number of exotic vacations helped the couple, whether to Martinique or to Italy. It was clearly time to confront not his wife but the other man.

His decision made, Alain entered the young chef's Pré Catelan second-floor office and calmly pointed outside to the parking lot, where the man could see a hunting rifle bag in Alain's car. This, he thought, established his seriousness. "You will resign from the company at once," he said. "You have all your mistresses, Catherine is nothing to you, but you are much too important to her. I am sorry, but you need to get out. Now."

The rival got the message and disappeared. Alain informed his parents he had fired the rival, without giving details. He had told them many times before that he had suspicions about the man. But there was no reaction then, and absolutely no support from his parents. Business was first for them.

Divorce is against the Catholic faith and was abhorrent to Alain. But he did not want to fall into a life of lying, as his parents had.

"My sisters and I had begged my parents to divorce so their fighting could stop," he told me several times. They did divorce, but only thirty years later. For his romantic life, Alain LeNôtre certainly did not consider his parents any kind of role model.

The decision to seek a divorce pressed on him, even though he was still in love with his wife—and even after a family counselor whom the couple had consulted informed him there was no hope of reconciliation. Alain would have forgiven everything if she had decided to return to him. But it was to no avail. Finally, Alain, heartbroken, instructed the LeNôtre family attorney to draw up and file the separation papers.

Catherine, who did not want to divorce, made the procedure last a long time but did not want to reconcile with Alain either. She had rented a house in the same neighborhood, allowing the kids to visit back and forth while remaining in the same school with the same sets of friends. And of course, above all, work went on for Alain and Catherine for the good of the LeNôtre Empire, like nothing had ever happened. Alain was devastated, his sister Sylvie told me later. In those days, Alain would go to work as usual, but the rest of the time he would be enclosed in his house, not going out, not seeing anyone, pale and unshaved like a hermit. We both, I came to understand, had gone through the same situation and felt the same pain.

A German coworker and friend in the LeNôtre export department to the German franchises, seeing Alain' loneliness and depression, suggested he consult the personal ads running in the magazine *Le Chasseur Français*. She told him that after her divorce, she had placed a four-line ad in it, had received three hundred letters, and soon after had remarried a very nice guy, a banker and a gentleman.

"I am very happy now," she told him with a big smile, "as you can see!"

Alain was touched by her confidence, but he did not follow her advice. And even as a distant cousin who had just remarried shared the same advice, he did not act. Only weeks later, after praying to God on his knees, and asking to find someone to love and be loved by, he was drawn to the magazine stand. It required but a few moments of paging through *Le Chasseur Français* before one ad caught his eye. In large type it read: SOS!

As a bride, in Colette's ermine cape

CHAPTER 8

You Can't Have Everything!

For years afterward, the most I told people about how I met Alain LeNôtre is that we had a "tennis date together." Like most of the best fibs, this was partially true. We did have a tennis date, as we were both members of the same sport club, Le Stade Français. What matters most is that we met.

Alain LeNôtre may have the same first name as my first husband, and even share April as a birth month, but it is impossible to overemphasize how different Alain Casau, romance, and marriage, were from Alain LeNôtre. We were so young the first time, of course, with no experience whatsoever of what marriage was all about: the things a mate should do or not do for the other, the constant watch of the fragile enterprise, the patience it takes, the commitment it requires. Our relationship never matured to form a solid bond based on mutual interests, beliefs and shared values. Whereas with Alain LeNôtre—no doubt helped along by the fact we were both betrayed and hurting, sharing the same experience, each one divorced with two children of virtually the same age—a deep friendship happened first. Our love started as a wonderful, gentle, and faithful friendship. For a time, even, I feared we'd have nothing more.

Not quite a week after Alain and I enjoyed our first date, he invited me to his house to celebrate his daughter's birthday with roast chicken, *pommes frites* and *desserts á la LeNôtre*. I knew I would go, and I knew I should go, but that didn't mean there were no nerves involved. It seemed serious to fall so early in our relationship but, as with so many things we did, our friendship made it feel like the right thing to do. At that time, my daughters were living with my ex and his new woman in Provence, so being with Alain's kids felt good to me in ways I wasn't yet ready to understand.

Catherine had moved out of the house and into her own place just a few doors away. The entire neighborhood was conceived much as an elegant American lakefront suburb with its pool, tennis courts, gardens and ponds. Later on, when we were married, this made for some rough times for me—since the proximity sometimes made it seem as though they were still together. However, the arrangement was excellent for Alain's children Cecile and Charles. Even though a schedule was established, they moved freely between the two houses, outside the official boundaries of whichever parent was supposed to have which child when. They were adorable kids, I decided that first day at the birthday party, and I tried my best to be friendly and natural around them so they would like me.

Once the party was over, the kids went off with their friends, and Alain and I played a little tennis—actually I had to endure his beginner's tennis, while I was *classée*, ranked. We settled close to the fireplace to talk, and finally I got up the nerve to tell him I had two kids, too. He was just fine with that. The more we talked, in fact, the more we realized how much we were suffering from the failure of our previous marriages and the more we fell naturally into helping each other as friends. There was a deep feeling of trust which permeated my entire being when I was with him, the feeling of being safe, saved, at peace. At long last, I had someone to talk to.

There was so much to do in Paris at this magical time in our romance. After all, the great Gaston LeNôtre was invited to anything and everything, and more often than not he was too busy to go. That meant Alain and I got the call, and, at least in the beginning, it was very exciting. From the opera to the ballet to the theater, we were there on opening nights, and also at the glittering social events that attended such high culture. I can remember sitting at many a table and seeing the likes of Henry Kissinger, Omar Sharif, Alain Delon, Margaux Hemingway, and Claudia Cardinale beside us or across from us. We traveled in the elevated circle that was LeNôtre. It was a thrill for me, a Greek from Athens, where few of these celebrities ever ventured beyond a trip to the beach.

When Alain started to turn up everywhere with me on his arm, the two of us always holding hands, everyone knew that Alain was separated from Catherine. I met his mother on the turf she ruled with an iron hand, Pré Catelan. I was impressed by her elegance, her demeanor of a woman in charge, and simply by who she was. Colette took one look at me over our tea and *petit fours* and pronounced, "Alain always did like blondes with long hair." I had trouble deciding what sort of compliment that was. But, overall, I found her charming, warm, and accepting.

As for Gaston, while I don't recall how we met the first time, I do remember that he quickly began acting like a father to me. Perhaps that was his nature as a man with a dozen family members already around—or perhaps as a paternalistic business owner with hundreds of employees—but it felt comforting when he was that way to me. At one of our first meetings he spotted me with a cigarette. "My dear, please don't smoke," he said. "It's not good for you." I have never picked up a cigarette since.

During the first weeks of our relationship, I invited Alain for dinner at my Opera flat and he brought me a box of LeNôtre pastries.

"Do you like them?" he asked, after I had taken a couple of bites.
"Well, not really, they are different," I replied.

"It is because you don't know," he snapped back.

The truth is I had not tried the LeNôtre pastries before, and I preferred Greek pastries. Good taste is acquired, developed, and I was a novice in the *haute* pastry department, obviously.

One of Gaston's recurring early themes was that I was so damn smart and pretty, what on earth was I doing with his son? He was such a charming flirtatious Frenchman, he seemed to be adding in silence "—and not with me?" As the weeks went by, I learned to diffuse his inquiries by telling him simply, "You don't know everything about Alain. He has qualities that surely you are unaware of."

As it happens, I was beginning to wonder the same kind of things myself. Alain was always gentle with me, no doubt projecting his own pained vulnerability onto the woman he was beginning to care about. In addition, he surely feared that if he tried to seduce me, to turn our friendship into an affair, he would risk losing me. We were frozen in place, and it worried me. I knew, as I told my mother during a phone conversation, that I'd met the man who had all the qualities I needed and could be a perfect husband. But it seemed we'd never move past holding hands and worse, that he might be impotent. My mother, as usual, was quick to answer my fears.

"It doesn't matter, after all," she said. "You can't have everything."

Many thoughts and revelations about Alain figured into this period. He felt, for instance, that Catherine had never truly loved him, that their marriage had been largely a sham to placate her parents. And if she had never loved him as a man, then no one had. We talked and we talked, about our disappointments in life, about our past grievances, but I suppose we never moved forward toward creating an "us" until I showed him he had my permission to do so. I remember we were in his car one evening, holding hands, when I did just a little more, stroking his fingers in a certain way, caressing his wrist. Alain certainly responded in kind. It was as though a great door long closed was flung open, and he dared to love me in a formidable way in return—at last. We made plans to marry that fall, on November tenth.

In preparation, a high school classmate from Athens who was in the city's fabled fashion industry took me to see a designer, Angelo Tarlazzi. He was probably looking to establish some sort of catering relationship with the LeNôtres, because he immediately agreed to dress me for the wedding—a loaner dress, much as Hollywood's biggest names borrow to attend the Oscars. I picked out a few possible colors (not white, since I'd been married before) and let the designer work his magic. I loved that fluffy maroon water silk *moire* dress and the beautiful shawl he put with it. Alain's mother draped an ermine cape around me before I went to church, so I wouldn't be cold. Oh, what a lovely gesture—but I returned the fur afterwards.

Alain and I said our vows at the old Greek Orthodox church in Paris, Rue Daru, his own Catholic church being closed to him because he was now divorced. In my church it is possible to re-marry four times, which gives a person a chance to make up his or her mind. For this service, he had to become Greek Orthodox, learning about the orthodox faith by attending a short seminar with the priest.

More than four hundred guests attended the dinner party at the Pré Catelan salons, after the church ceremony. From Greece came my parents, of course, along with my sister Neny and a couple of my friends from high school. At the appointed hour, a towering six-layer wedding cake escorted by our four children was carried out by waiters in tuxedos, as though they were transporting some ancient ruler. At the top there was a representation of the bride and groom—in blown sugar, surrounded by four kids, dancing the *farandole*. The master of ceremonies clapped his hands and two perfect white doves burst from inside the cake and circled overhead.

We opened the ball with our first waltz. At midnight, the traditional music of France was replaced by Greek dances played on *bouzoukia* and led by my Greek friend, Jenny Roucher, who'd studied ballet at the Athens Opera. She and her French husband Gilles were our best man and woman. No one could resist the traditional *sirtaki* dance—the whole room filling with sudden, not-always-coordinated Zorbas—Colette and Gaston joining my parents with great amusement.

Gaston invited us on a business trip to Tokyo, which at the same time would serve as our honeymoon. Business was business. The purpose of the trip was to expand the franchise from seven to fourteen stores. After the successful business negotiations with the Seibu people were over, we escaped to visit the ancient capital, Kyoto. We opted to stay at a traditional Japanese hotel where we had to sleep on a mat on the floor, with a geisha on her knees watching from her dark corner, ready to tend to our slightest need. We could not speak Japanese and never did manage to get her out of our bedroom to have some privacy, so our honeymoon was ruined. And at first we hesitated to wash, as the bathroom was communal, with no running water. There were only wooden buckets to dip into a warm water tank below the wooden floor. We finally did wash, while fearing that at any moment a stranger would walk in.

When we returned, we settled in as husband and wife at his house in Plaisir, and all four kids became good friends. By then I had quit my job at the travel agency, since I knew there would be more than enough in motherhood to keep me busy. It felt wonderful to have my own daughters, Nathalie and Armelle, back with me. I'd missed them so much. When they'd first met Alain at the airport for Easter vacations, their rosy faces turned pleasantly surprised. Alain was tender and affectionate with them, offering each a beautiful doll. He then told them on the side, "You know I love your mother very much!"

"*Et bien tant mieux,*" Armelle responded, holding hands firmly with her sister. "That's good news!"

They were now both part of the daily swirl that included school, piano lessons, tennis, catechism and of course homework. Alain was off working, but this time things were different. I encouraged him to go back to school and get an executive MBA at the University of Paris, as I thought that would complement all the empirical knowledge he had amassed working in his father's business, and he did it during the weekends. By the end of 1981, he convinced his class of eighty graduates to take the traditional end-of-class trip to Brazil, instead of Japan, and I made sure to accompany the group. Otherwise he could not go, I told the president of the MBA student association.

"We've just been married," I said, "and I let him spend our Saturdays at school. But I will not let him go to Brazil alone!"

I now carried the name LeNôtre, and that from the start propelled me to places I'd never dreamed of going—and in some cases, to places that I'd never particularly wanted to go. There was hunting, for instance, which Gaston took with incredible seriousness both as business and as pleasure. But being Gaston, he mostly combined hunting with business. Virtually every weekend in the fall, he expected Alain, me, and our children to come to their luxurious hunting property beside a lake and surrounded by forests, all to help him entertain the heads of major international corporations who were his highest-end catering clients and friends

I had never hunted, and at first the entire business seemed strange. Everything was formed around food and drink, from *paté* and hard apple cider in the morning to magnificent feasts for dinner. Gaston sat in the middle of everything when the guests gathered for meals at his U-shaped table in the living room. When he wasn't putting the arm on a specific president or CEO, he often invited me to sit next to him.

Some of the celebrities came from the world of food and wine. Paul Bocuse visited more than once, and even Robert Mondavi came from California. I still have our photograph with the man who invented the modern California wine industry. For the hunts, all guests would be outfitted by the LeNôtres with boots, hats, coats, amid the snarling and barking of excited hunting dogs. At last the group would take to the fields, forest, and lakes, ready to blast away at their limit of duck, pheasant, wild boar, and deer, depending on the season. Sometimes I would have preferred a relaxing weekend at our house, but these weekends meant big business for Gaston. When it came to hunting with Gaston, it was always a command performance. Eventually, I took lessons in shooting, so I could participate in the ritual.

Another way to participate came during our first holiday season after the wedding. As many know about retail and catering, I suddenly realized I might not lay eyes on my husband until early January, so I volunteered instead to help out at one of the boutiques, Avenue de Wagram near the Champs-Élysées. I was given a modicum of training, both front and back of the house, then unleashed on unsuspecting customers. Everyone knew who I was, and everyone was quick to show respect. But in the end, all the staff worked side-by-side with me.

There was no time for pecking order during the crush of holiday preparation. I'll never forget when Colette and even Gaston himself made the rounds, shaking employees' hands and thanking them for all their hard work. Employees were in awe of these two, and it showed in the way they never stopped, even when they were exhausted. When we'd finally filled the last order on the last day, it was three or perhaps four in the morning. All of us gathered behind the scenes for a generous celebration built around *foie gras* and champagne. I was honored when the next holiday season rolled around and I was asked to work in the shops again.

About this time, though, an entirely new, entirely daunting ambition had begun to form within the LeNôtres. For one thing, there was the state of things in France—where a socialist-communist government had Alain and his parents afraid that the entire family fortune might be at great risk. For another, there was the opportunity always implied by the very word "America." The idea, born of discussions with a possible franchise investor, was to launch a chain of branded LeNôtre pastry boutique in all the major American cities.

I was for it from day one. My mother had been born in New York. And while I'd never actually visited America, I knew of its many quirks and wonderments from a lifetime of watching American movies. After eighteen months of married life in Paris, as Gaston wondered who could run his gutsy American subsidiary, I cornered Alain and simply said, "Let's go."

From the outside looking in, marriage to the heir apparent of the Gaston LeNôtre culinary fortune would have surely looked privileged, even easy enough to be the cause of envy. I could not know at the time—and indeed even Alain had barely started to recognize the fact—that the fortune was entering its most challenging and dangerous period ever. But now, as Alain and I settled into married life, the drama was being played out on a far bigger stage, with a far bigger fortune to lose.

In retrospect, a lot of the difficulties to come grew directly from Gaston's own personality: his greatest weaknesses sprouting from his greatest strengths. The same pull he felt from success and the adulation of everyone old enough to cook or even eat in France would, increasingly over his later years, leave him vulnerable to anyone willing to flatter him round the clock. The way to take advantage of Gaston, and perhaps make off with the empire he'd built, was to appeal to the image he held of himself.

In the course of the breakup with Catherine, Alain had not made his dealings with his parents any easier by confronting them about Catherine's lover and the situation that Gaston and Colette had fostered by welcoming the young chef into the family. The fact that this "adopted son," Catherine's lover, had ruined their real son Alain's marriage and caused him great suffering from which he'd never completely recover, seemed amazingly unimportant to Gaston and Colette. Later, when the young chef married a national television anchor in France, Gaston and Colette hosted a massive society ball at Pré Catelan for the happy couple—no doubt seeking media coverage, but oblivious to the hurt it caused Alain.

I suppose their business empire, their reputation, and the formidable energy behind it could not be undermined by silly sentimentalities of that order from their son. I am sure they felt Alain was weak, fragile—not like them! Business mattered more than anything—this is how they succeeded in the first place. Their children would be part of the big adventure only if they helped it to move forward, no matter what.

This young and charismatic chef, Alain's rival, besides being talented, he had been adopted by both Gaston and Colette for different reasons. Colette was sensitive to his obvious sexual charms and Gaston was amused with the entire situation of *ménage à trois* and sultry extramarital affairs. These two, Gaston and Colette, needed to have some fun too while working so hard to succeed, and they did!

I suspect this dramatic episode for Alain propelled his parents to want him out of their immediate entourage. Having Alain married again and happy, they sensed he was less needed in France, so that they could do as they pleased. Alain had always been the watchdog for his parents, over business schemes or foul friendships, therefore we had their blessings to embark for America. As for me, I wanted the big adventure. America meant that everything was possible. America meant a new life of our own, Alain and I. The truth is, with all the glamour and indulgent social life, big parties, fancy restaurants, and being a LeNôtre, I felt suffocated, oppressed in some way by the family burden. I longed for fresh air. I longed for independence. America was the new Paris for me, a new world to explore.

The promise of America beckoned us, as did the idea of showing the family we could create something wonderful and profitable on our own. But it would take the Bible story, or at least some combination of Sigmund Freud and Herman Melville, to tell the story that unfolded of the betrayal of this son by the father he sought only to please.

There was a prelude to our decision to launch in America: the LeNôtres' serious discussion with yet another franchised operation, this one in Mexico. We were invited by the Martell Corporation to visit Mexico City to explore a joint venture to help them promote their Mexican/French Cognac business.

Here we were, Alain and I, Gaston and Colette, returning from one of those late-night Mexican hacienda dinners, arriving at our hotel at midnight. We planned to get up at 4 a.m. to visit the city central market from which we'd be getting food for our future operation. What we didn't know as we went to bed was that a fire had already started in one of the hotel's banquet rooms; no alarm was activated for evacuation. When we were awakened by smoke rushing in under the bedroom door, we discovered the dark side of staying in the Presidential Suite. Due to concerns for security, there was no way out. Alain, having been an Eagle Scout in his youth, brought us outside into a small enclosed courtyard and began climbing up a decorative wall to look for a possible escape from the roof. He went the first time on his own, after his parents had refused, then returned and convinced us we should follow him.

Once there, still fearful the building would be consumed in flames or simply crumble beneath us in the intense heat, we at last spotted a group of passersby four floors beneath who eventually called the fire truck. After one ladder proved too short and another started out parked in the opposite direction, Gaston, Colette and I managed to climb down to safety. Alain, however, refused to leave the roof, having noticed a couple trapped in the neat courtyard. The husband had a broken leg. Alain, always the Boy Scout and Good Samaritan, ran to point out the couple. Before he was able to do so, Alain, still in his underwear and barefoot, was tackled by the fireman. He fell and broke his ankle.

When he was treated that night in the emergency room of the Red Cross hospital in Mexico City, he found himself in a bed next to the man he'd helped to save. The following day however, we did visit as planned the magnificent museum of natural sciences, with me pushing Alain in his wheelchair. This experience, along with our witnessing the lack of safety procedure and professional management in the best hotel in the country's capital, which caused the death of three employees, made us decide not to pursue business in that country.

The idea of launching the LeNôtre brand in the United States had started out in earnest in 1975 on 59th Street, near Bloomingdales in New York City, with a French franchisee from Bernay in Normandy. A poor contract was signed by Gaston alone, who did not get advice from any business lawyer, consultant or family member. Against Gaston's advice, the franchisee hired a director, who managed to sink the well-publicized and promising project. Everybody in New York was talking about this in dismay, wondering why such a fine place, inaugurated with great fanfare with the presence of chefs Michel Guérard and Paul Bocuse (and a Normand cow tied on the sidewalk facing the *pâtisserie* and restaurant) had closed after two years of commercial success.

Gaston, vexed, had to make some sort of retaliation. But he was not sure if this should be organized as a company-owned subsidiary or a franchise. Nevertheless, there was already a franchisee in the new discussions, an Iranian *émigré* who'd served the Shah as finance minister before the Ayatollah's revolution. We had the option of using that "money guy," Gaston said. Alain and I were sent to America to investigate which strategy to use and where.

This time, Gaston hired an American business attorney and a French consultant, a former manager of Yves Saint Laurent outlets and franchises in the US, to plan the exploratory trip and escort us. Even though the Iranian wanted to invest only in the Sunbelt, the consultant designed a trip through New York, Chicago, San Francisco, Los Angeles, Dallas, and Miami, all the hot fashion megalopolises he knew, I suppose. In Manhattan, Monsieur Dumas Hermès kindly received us at the Hermès headquarters. He warned us of the danger and difficulty of the US market, from his own experience.

"Is there one city in the US," Alain asked, "where Hermès is not yet that could be your next location?" The man's response was immediate: Houston.

Alain's executive MBA-style brain was wary of northern weather conditions, as they might often hamper those essential air and land deliveries. There were also the costs (most of them hidden) of doing business in the Rust Belt, where labor unions were likely to exert huge power over such a labor-intensive business. And then there were the economic realities of the early 1980s, when Texas enjoyed the fastest-growing economy of any state in the union and Houston enjoyed the fastest growth in Texas. The subtropical weather was attractive, a busy international community with ninety consulates, an international airport, a French high school, and an underpinning of affluence and enjoyment that spoke well to the LeNôtre luxury brand.

Finally, in that way that little things can make a big difference when you let them, Alain had made a survey of the Ecole LeNôtre alumni in the United States, and there were two former students living in Houston—meaning there were at least two people we could visit and interrogate about the city. Even though our return flight to France was pressing upon us, we insisted to our consultant that we wouldn't leave without a quick trip to Houston.

We had a warm Texas welcome from those former students and their contacts in Houston. With less than two days to spend, we committed an extravagance by chartering a helicopter to fly us over the city. That was one way to see Houston in the least amount of time. I remember how impressed we were with the view from above the graceful streets, the active glass-and-steel business district downtown, the Medical Center (largest in the world), NASA, Galveston Island and the retail-crazed Galleria. We couldn't believe the number of homes that had in-ground swimming pools, since in France movie stars were practically the only people who had those.

One of our most important contacts in Houston proved to be luxury department store owner Bob Sakowitz. We hit it off with Bob immediately, not least because he spoke fluent French. We quickly moved from warm welcome to business possibilities. Bob's customers, including those wealthy and beautiful ladies who lunch after buying his furs, were our customers too, and we could envision setting up LeNôtre boutique's within the five Sakowitz stores. Bob certainly had plans to open even more, answering in his own Houston way the challenge set out by Neiman Marcus up in Dallas. During our following trip, this time with Gaston himself, Bob invited us to a party in the wine cellar at his house, honoring English designer Zandra Rhodes, introducing us at the same time to the society fixtures Houston considered important.

Following our US tour, Alain's original plan for the family was to create a national chain of shops selling only ice cream and ice cream cakes made in a LeNôtre US commissary, along with fine chocolate candies imported from the newly acquired LeNôtre chocolate factory at Tinchebray in Normandy, a kind of Godiva and Häagen-Dazs combination. But Gaston dismissed Alain's idea and insisted that he duplicate the full Parisian model of boutiques (with extensive lines of sweet and savory products), building on the LeNôtre Parisian reputation and the earlier success with the German and Japanese franchises.

Alain was instructed to cobble together a business model with a single centrally located commissary and approximately twenty boutiques. They were to be opened in affluent locations in major US cities, perhaps in the Sunbelt as the Iranian franchisee candidate suggested. The idea would be to produce frozen, uncooked Danishes, croissants, macaroons, pastries, breads, *pâtés*, appetizers, ice cream, and ice cream cakes in a central production outlet, then rush them daily by air or freezer truck to each boutique. Many would require proofing, baking, and decoration onsite. This was what was done in Paris, and Gaston was sure it would work in the United States.

After our US exploration in 1981, we had lots to report to the family board back home; and some of it marked a dramatic change from what they expected to hear. Most importantly, after learning of the challenges facing French companies like Hermès and Yves Saint Laurent in the US, Alain advised that direct franchising was simply not the way to go or grow in America. There was too much risk of lawsuits, which were very common in the US Control had to remain with the family, he said, in the interest of sheer quality control. And that meant organizing ourselves as a Master Franchisee.

The investment to build the central headquarters and commissary had to come from the family, along with the close-knit cadre of Gaston's hunting buddies, who were already LeNôtre minority investors. The vision, looking back, was formed before Mitterand's election, when LeNôtre France still had enough cash flow for the project and there was still the possibility of bank loans, if we needed them, as well as franchise opportunity once the pilot stores could be shown as profitable.

That's what we knew. What Gaston didn't know (or did not want to see) could have killed us. He didn't yet realize the impact of the new socialist/communist government that would come to France in 1982 under President François Mitterrand and was about to wreak havoc on the country's economy by creating the 35-hour workweek, nationalizing 100% of French banks and freezing prices.

All of our budgetary plans were based on the then-current exchange rate of five French francs (there were no euros in those days) to the American dollar, and that rate was soon diminished by almost half—virtually doubling the investment required for the American adventure. We also didn't realize that Gaston himself was embarking—again, without any discussion with Alain—on a series of investments in Paris, Geneva, Orlando, and Montreal that would undermine the entire family's financial security.

One was a lavish remodeling of the headquarters in Plaisir, which Alain had already ushered so carefully through six expansions. Another was the purchase of Gaston's longtime dream, a restaurant along the lines of Pré Catelan on the Champs-Elysées, near the Place de la Concorde facing the presidential Élysées Palace. It was to be called LeNôtre Elysée. Talk about "location, location, location." But the acquisition, which was supposed to cost seven million francs (then about $1 million) with the remodeling, and an additional wine cellar ended up tying up 20 million francs.

Also, Yves Piaget, the famous jeweler and a regular at Pré Catelan, had seduced Gaston into opening a LeNôtre boutique in Geneva as a 50/50 joint venture. Alain visited the Swiss city, did some market research, and wrote a report, recommending against the venture. His advice was ignored, and the boutique lasted less than two years. And there was, for Gaston, the ultimate vanity project: the creation of the Chefs de France Pavilion at Disney's EPCOT in Orlando.

This behavior was becoming the norm, and even though Alain was supposed to have the US and Canada as his territory, Gaston entered talks with Disney alongside his buddies Bocuse and Verger for the fun of it. The EPCOT French Pavillon with its three restaurants, LeNôtre pastry shop, a French souvenir boutique and a 360-degree movie theatre, would, as we all knew, become the LeNôtre family's highest-profile project in the United States. Plus, since the deal was set up with most costs falling upon its partners, EPCOT tied up even more of the family's money that should have gone into our Texas subsidiary.

We didn't realize any of this until the EPCOT grand opening, which included two Concorde supersonic planes landing in Orlando with the chefs, their staff and many VIP guests from all over France.

As we now know, this is where the stretched finances of company and family would ultimately play such a dangerous and damaging role. Alain was elected by the board to become the president of the new US subsidiary. He accepted on the condition that we would have 35% of that company's stock in return for our personal cash investment, which came from the sale of his home and my apartment in Paris. Typical of French commerce, and especially of family businesses, a simple one-page contract was drawn up, outlining not who would do what and get what but only Alain's compensation. Everybody signed. The Iranian investor was dismissed, and the great migration to America began.

CHAPTER 8: YOU CAN'T HAVE EVERYTHING

The blessing of the bread during the LeNôtre Paris headquarters opening, 1983

Chef Gaston LeNôtre

CHAPTER 9

Our Beautiful Profession

W e flew to Houston and stayed in the Omni Hotel on Woodway, with our four kids— they had a great time, drinking Coca-Cola at will, watching movies in their beds and splashing in the warm pool waters graced by the black swans. In the meantime, I toured at least one hundred homes in two weeks and found a five-bedroom charming house with a cathedral ceiling in Hedwig village, very near Memorial High School. My real estate agent would spend the entire day with me visiting houses in the Memorial area—this is where she advised we should live. We would stop for lunch, a salad or quiche, and continue the showings the entire afternoon. Most of the houses then were old, yet large compared to European standards. They had extensive lawns, but nothing new was built in 1982 when we arrived.

Our house was the newest in the neighborhood and our kids loved the crescent shaped pool, with its diving board, the basketball hoop, and the pecan trees. The squirrels were fun to watch hiding or eating their acorns. What was not fun were the huge roaches flying from the trees and into our home. I had never seen any that size before except in Iguasu Falls, in Brazil. Our Vietnamese maid, Lin tried to save them from extermination by picking them up alive and throwing them back into the garden.

Lin was our second maid. The first, Betty had abruptly left after she discovered I was pregnant with our son Gaston. This is how the story goes.

A year into my marriage, my mother had started pestering me again.

"You should have another baby," she said, matter-of-factly.

"Why? " I asked. "I am happy beyond words, and we don't need another child. We have four already."

"Nevertheless," my mother said, "you do need to consolidate your marriage with a child. This is the way it is. Trust me. And you are not getting any younger, either."

I thought about it for a while. My daughters, Nathalie eleven, and Armelle nine, were living with me then, along with Charles nine, and Cecile twelve. They got along perfectly, we had a housemaid, and everything was under control. *So do I want another child?* I pondered. *Yes,* a voice in the back of my head said, *But only if it were a boy.*

A boy in my family was a rare commodity. My mother had four girls. She lost the only boy she gave birth to during the war, when he was only a few months old. A boy was my mother's dream, and she had infused it to me by osmosis. I started searching the literature and books about choosing the sex of a child. And I went to see a specialist, again!

His name was Jean Choucroun. He had pioneered a research based on nutrition, I was told, with 80% success rate for women who followed his diet strictly. He was confident that he could deal with my problem—my several problems actually, he added, after he examined my chart.

"You are thirty-seven years old," he said, "and that is not an optimum age for a pregnancy. You have only one Fallopian tube working due to your earlier ectopic pregnancy. And you have a family history of producing girls. All this is quite challenging."

"We will overcome all that, you and me," I said. "I trust your expertise, and I will behave. Just give me the orders. I will do everything it takes to have a boy."

He provided me with a specific diet, based on the research he had done previously with farm animals, cows in particular. His regimen was a high salt diet consisting of ham, bacon, beans, avocados, bananas, and oranges. Dairy products, shellfish, and nuts were forbidden.

"Your husband must abide to it as well," he said. "It will help you and your couple's equilibrium. You need his support to succeed."

Alain had no problem following my diet, and we'd stuck to it for a year or so, no matter what Colette and Gaston thought of our strange ways of eating. By then it was 1982 and we'd moved to Texas. I had stuck with the diet religiously, plus I had incorporated some new tricks to reinforce my chances.

After a few months in the US my American doctor called me with the big news: "You are 100% pregnant, and it's a boy," he said. "He even has a big nose!"

"Heavens!" I said. "A big nose!"

I ran into the house to call Alain, and I bumped into our maid. "I am pregnant with a boy," I cried to her. "A boy, you hear? It is a well- deserved miracle!"

The maid, Betty, was tall and stiff. She looked at me bewildered and went directly to her room, shaking her head. The next thing I knew, she appeared with her suitcase in hand.

"I could not handle another child in here. I am done with you, French!" she said dismissively and walked straight through the front door. She was unhappy in our house, I knew. She had to iron (she gave her own clothing to the dry cleaners), and she had to buy her own Coca-cola, as we did not allow it in our house. *Et voila!* This is how we replaced Betty with our French speaking maid, Lin.

By then, I had enrolled the kids at the Awty International School, which featured a bilingual French curriculum, and started looking for land to buy for our headquarters. Houston was a foreign country, for sure. The men at the airport were tanned, working in shorts and baseball hats. The odd smell of the summer humidity took us by surprise—we could not breathe. The pine trees were a tapestry of green, luxurious green, and everything was so clean. People were smiling at the bank or the grocery store, so different from the Parisians. Lawn mowers were running every morning everywhere we turned. My God, I thought, why do they need to clean every pavement or sidewalk every day?

For our headquarters, we found the perfect property, we thought, perched alongside I-45 eight minutes north of downtown, a reasonably quick jaunt from the Bush Intercontinental Airport. Perhaps most importantly, the building for the company would have high visibility to the 250,000 car commuters who headed north or south each day between Houston and the affluent Woodlands development created by fellow Greek George Mitchell. Next, we called on a French-fluent California business attorney we'd met at Pré Catelan, one who also represented a major construction company in Houston.

Alain drew up his own layout for what was needed to satisfy Gaston's desire for a large product line such as in the family's Paris shops. Then we hired an Italian/French architect to make it all official.

Downstairs in the glass-and-steel building would be the manufacturing area incorporating a model LeNôtre boutique with many counters—one for cakes, one for croissants and Danishes, one for individual pastries and tarts, one for chocolate candies, one for ice cream, and ice cream cakes, one for rolls and bread, and finally one for charcuterie, *pâté* and deli. We obtained a USDA license. Upstairs would be a training center, intended to prepare significant employees for LeNôtre boutiques in what would soon be many American cities. Alain carefully drew in where each piece of cooking and baking equipment made absolute sense, using his operational knowledge and even added a striking glass loop corridor running throughout. We were getting ready.

We then looked for many possible places to open outlets in the French bakery café style. We signed two leases in Houston—one with Sakowitz on Post Oak at Westheimer, one on Memorial Drive at Town and Country Village. We visited Dallas extensively and signed two leases there, one in Northpark Mall and the other in the Sakowitz store in North Dallas. Alain designed the layout of the four places as well, hired a well-established French interior decorator and ordered the equipment for both production and the stores. The elegant showcases were imported from Italy—ah, those Italians, beautiful design dwells right in their hearts.

We had the plant and headquarter designs converted into blueprints and presented for a bid to the concrete construction company acting as general contractor. When we got the bid, it seemed fair and more or less what we were expecting. And that's when Gaston, who had barely visited Houston, started putting his foot down. Alain asked him to transfer the funds set aside for the entire project, as agreed, but Gaston declined, saying he had bought certificates of deposit with the money on favorable terms. Each time we needed money, he said, we just had to ask. Actually the money was coming so slowly that we had to arrange a loan from two French banks doing business in Houston to finance the purchase of the land and the plant construction.

The bid for the plant was too high, Gaston fumed. Eventually, though, it slowly became clear to us that the real problem was not the amount but the lack of available money. Yet Gaston remained an eternal optimist, the kind of guy who'd survived the war in Normandy while having the Gestapo as his next-door neighbor and escaped forced labor deportation in Germany. You survive something like that and you think any challenge can be overcome. But now, to our dismay, little by little we discovered the family's dire financial straits.

Gaston reviewed the set of blueprints, he set about moving this here or there, cutting out this or that to save a few dollars. Two versions followed the first version, each set costing additional time and money. The opening was set for September 1983. We missed that date by two months, primarily because of delays in the permits, brought about by Gaston's continual redesigns.

Back in France, throughout the Houston building process,

Gaston followed the advice of another "hunting friend" and investment banker, who convinced him to replace Alain in France and in Texas with a general manager from his own bank staff. But of course! Considering his immense financial difficulties, Gaston was left with no choice but to accept. It was the 1980s, and the world was only beginning to learn about "takeover artists." That was, more or less, what was afoot among the LeNôtres in Paris, with affable PR guy Gaston listening more and more to the flattery of "friends" who would eventually lead to his downfall. Even worse, all the financial troubles brought about by Gaston's poor judgment mixed with France's poor economy were about to be blamed on us.

Alain, who had committed his career of twenty years to his family, to being "the good son," now had to suffer the indignity of having his own father try to push him out. The pressure came from several fronts: First, Gaston needed a scapegoat for the delay in opening the US operation and its subsequent costs. And of course he did not want to share credit with us for generating so much media about the family's venture in Houston. I remember when I showed him a three-page color spread story of Alain and myself I was so proud to have obtained in the *Houston Post*.

"Why did you not wait for my arrival to get that interview?" he told me, frowning and dismissive. "I am the one who does PR in this company."

He was upset to miss an opportunity to be in the headlines of US papers himself. Another push came from the outside. There were preludes to this, naturally, mostly focused on Gaston's constant effort during each US visit to reduce our 35% ownership of the American subsidiary, now nearing the opening of its main headquarters, as well as of three retail stores in Houston and two in Dallas.

Gaston's investment banker friend and his new general manager turned up at our house one day, allegedly to see how the preparations were going. They offered Alain a "golden parachute," approved by Gaston himself. That was a one-time payment if he'd leave his position. "Accepting this would be good for Alain, good for the company and good for the family," the document said. Despite being traumatized by his family's betrayal, Alain read through the two-page addendum to his one-page contract and signed.

A month after the signature of the golden parachute, a formal meeting with his father, mother, and two sisters was organized at an upper floor office at the Four Seasons Hotel. As a non-direct part of the family, I was not invited. At that hotel meeting, we were simply fired. All Alain remembers today is looking out to the balcony with its low wall, thinking about how easy it would be to walk out and jump to his death.

With us out of the way, Gaston could keep 100% of his company stock, and 100% of the fame, for himself. In one of the most outlandishly insensitive sidebars to that entire part of the LeNôtre saga, even as Gaston was removing us from the company, he was asking me to arrange for the grand opening reception in our production center, with him at the head of it. After all, I had met and courted all the media in Houston and indeed across Texas—and Gaston demanded nothing for his grand presence as much as media. I agreed, of course.

We staged a kick-off dinner party for the March of Dimes for 300 well-heeled Houstonians. Gaston had the chocolates, champagne, and fresh orchids flown in from Paris—money did not seem to be a problem now. Our building was packed with black-tied men and elegant women in long dresses.

I wore my green silk Lanvin dress and a big smile. Robert Mondavi donated the wine and, even better, attended with his second wife Margrit. Bob Sakowitz was there, providing a bitter-sweet reminder of the warm welcome Houston had given Alain and me when we had first chosen it from all other American cities to be our home, less than two years before.

For all attending our extravagant event in February of 1984, it was a glorious beginning. For me and Alain, the ever-faithful son—it was the end.

By the time the legendary Gaston LeNôtre gathered his Houston employees to inform them that we would be leaving the company, it was impressive to see how much we had to leave. In only a year and a half, we had financed and completed construction of the 28,000 sqf plant on I-45, along with three high-profile boutiques in Houston and two in Dallas. We had also hired and trained 70 employees. It was to these employees, who had joined the company at Alain's invitation and based on their intuitive faith in him, that the now sixty-plus-year-old Gaston delivered his remarks entirely in French with a translator.

To this day, Alain keeps a copy of his father's typed remarks. Gaston praised us, for instance, for taking on the "great mission" of bringing the LeNôtre brand to North America. According to his presentation, Alain and I had decided to go into business for ourselves, to find new retail outlets for Houston-made LeNôtre pastries in California. "In this way," the great man told employees, some of whom were in tears by this point, "my son will remain my faithful *collaborateur*, associate."

In what must have been a sentimental moment, Gaston fell back on every aging Frenchman's fantasy: the notion of an eternal dynasty that carries on the great name.

"It would be your infant son Gaston Junior, born in Houston in 1983, he read from his paper, "who might someday run this US company I hope," he continued, "that I might live long enough to see my grandson and namesake working in our beautiful profession."

We would have to forget, Alain and I, how little he'd cared about his own son doing precisely that. And typical of such announcements to people counting on their paychecks, Gaston promised that his own management would "not create any dramatic change."

The idea that Alain and I would open our own business, as Gaston envisioned, was unthinkable to us then. It had never crossed Alain's mind to quit the family business. He felt he would succeed his father when the time came and he felt that he was utterly prepared for that; his position as deputy general manager, his experience dealing with every issue of manufacturing, selling, building, negotiating, and creating franchised operations. We were heartbroken. Crushed to the ground. Day after day we pondered our future together, judging the situation, the markets and trends. We thought about California. My sister Athena Debusk lived in Los Angeles, which could be handy, I thought. We have always been close, and she and her husband Michael invited us to visit.

We flew to Los Angeles and found an impressive space for a LeNôtre boutique on Rodeo Drive. Anticipating poor economic conditions (though hardly along Rodeo Drive), Gaston wrote to his attorney / business advisor in California to cease this particular search. "Alain," he wrote, "can open something for himself. But no LeNôtre franchise boutique will be opened in Los Angeles. That's it." We accepted the verdict.

We returned to Houston in time to celebrate Christmas with our children, who had been staying in our house on Memorial with their nanny. Really, we weren't sure how much we had to celebrate. But we tried to keep a happy face for our children who were our only treasures—we knew that well. And being together reinforced our family. They might have sensed the big turmoil with the LeNôtre, I bet they did, but they protected us from the outside world. Both Alain's and my children had adopted their brother, our little Gaston, and competed over who was going to feed him, read to him, play with him. Our children were our blessing and safety in the tornado that swept our professional world away.

There were ironies in all of this. Alain's sister Annie, at Gaston's request, came over from Paris to help run the five boutiques in Houston and Dallas after we were ousted. But Annie spoke little English, which made running anything in America pretty much impossible. We invited Annie to stay at our house. Family would always be family.

By April, less than three months after all the publicity of our grand opening, the money from Paris ran out—and the operation was still far from paying its own way. It became apparent to us that it was better for the takeover artists if the company went broke, in America and even in France, with a domino effect. Once that happened, they could acquire LeNôtre for little money. These were the people Gaston had trusted with his legacy.

Gaston became unable to find solutions, even temporary solutions, and in the end, they brought in a large French company called Accord, best known for its hotel brand Sofitel, to buy LeNôtre. The investment banker and Gaston kept us away, both from the assets themselves and from competing successfully with whatever version of the US LeNôtre would emerge from the fray. They would have done anything, it seemed, to keep us out.

Regarding our plant building, the new controlling partners actually paid a French competitor in Houston $1.5 million to take ownership of the plant and assume the payments on the mortgage. There seemed to be no specific plans to use our facility, and all we saw was that the competitor received $1.5 million and sold all the equipment including the pieces in the five stores before vanishing from Texas. Following the fall of the price of oil from $70 to $7 a barrel, Texas banks were closing right and left. Office towers downtown and elsewhere stood half-empty at best. Within a couple years in the mid-1980s, upwards of 300- to 400,000 people moved away from Houston. After this competitor's disappearance, the bank repossessed the building and sold it for a mere $300,000 to a Chinese investor living in Houston.

The place was virtually a shell by this point. And with all the LeNôtre retail outlets closed, there was not even a place to sell anything that might possibly be baked within those walls again.

Interestingly, neither Alain's original one-page agreement nor his two-page "golden parachute" contained what many American contracts put front and center—a specific non-compete clause, with specific definitions and durations. It was about this time that creating a cooking school in Houston first entered our minds. We still kept in contact with three of the now-former chefs from France who wanted to stay in Houston. There was certainly no culinary school in Texas—and arguably in the US—exactly like what Alain had created in Plaisir. And with the local economy such a disaster, there might be an opportunity to base the school in some under-utilized hotel, we thought, rather than buying or building a place of our own again. Things sounded promising at the start, not least because students could stay in the chosen hotel at a reduced nightly rate, making the school what Americans love to call a win-win operation. However, we never did manage to close such a deal.

Then, one day, the phone rang. The voice on the other end of the line belonged to a famously successful Houston grocer and wholesaler. He had a proposition for us.

Alain and I promote our own Town & Country Bakery
cafe opening, 1985

CHAPTER 10

How The Cookie Crumbled

> *Life is a long lesson in humility.*
>
> **JAMES M. BARRIE**

"A lain," Albert Jamail said over the phone. "I learned that your father's business has folded and he closed the stores.** What a pity. I want you to open a French bakery in my supermarket."

We were flattered, naturally. And certainly the fact that Albert Jamail was a Lebanese-American businessman who had created Houston's favorite luxury food retailer made such an arrangement seem logical. The ladies of River Oaks and Tanglewood socialized at Jamail's, many charging their purchases to personal accounts that produced a bill only once a year. The family-owned business loved the idea of welcoming another family-owned business, in this case Alain and me. Still, after some quick calculations about the space he'd toured, Alain said there wouldn't be enough square footage for what such a high-end bakery would need.

"Oh, that's this spot," said Albert, pulling out a thick roll of blueprints. "I want you in this extension I am planning for my store."

Within two weeks, we'd agreed to open a French bakery in the new, improved, and enlarged Jamail's. Albert would handle

———— *139* ————

the investment in infrastructure, and we would bring in our own equipment. At that point, having seen all the LeNôtre equipment sold, stolen, or both, we would have to start that process from scratch. And while we were working toward the Jamail's boutique, we realized something else. Ten months before, since neither money nor paperwork had arrived in time, we had leased the Town and Country boutique space on Memorial Drive in our own name. We'd had no choice then, but now it meant the lease was still technically and legally ours.

We pointed out the specifics to the landlord, and he agreed. The Town and Country store became the first of our bakery-cafés to open, followed shortly thereafter by Jamail's, using our own name—Alain & Marie LeNôtre Bakery, LeNôtre being the same size as Alain & Marie. We had no right to use the LeNôtre name alone anymore for our bakeries. Bob Sakowitz heard about our efforts and invited us to resuscitate the LeNôtre operation in his store as well. A Voss and Woodway bakery café opened later. That made a total of four outlets, a number that increased to seven when we were asked to create pastry shops in three local Macy's stores. One thing was becoming clear. We needed a plant. We needed to set up a baking operation somewhere.

During our first Houston dinner at the Sakowitz home, we'd met and made friends with Frank Malone and his wife, Rosemary. Frank, was already a familiar fixture around the city's chefs and restaurants, having built Tony's and, farther out west, Rotisserie for Beef and Bird with Joe Manke.

We found a shell of a building to lease on Bingle off I-10 and turned that into a baking operation. We started baking with three of the chefs we'd brought from France for LeNôtre, but two were hired away by the takeover artists in Paris, who we felt were still trying to undermine our modest start. Happily, we were able to locate a third LeNôtre veteran Chef, Etienne Corbet, a fine pastry maker, who was loyal and honest and stayed with us for ten years.

Finally divorced from the LeNôtre corporate nightmare, we had no choice but to operate the plant and especially its retail outlets as a small, virtually penniless, family business. Indeed, by the time we paid all our employees, there was nothing left. I often found myself making deliveries or standing in the stores selling croissants, baking cookies, making samples for customers, opening or closing stores. And when things went wrong, we showed ourselves to be a family business indeed.

Armelle, Charles, and Nathalie, now teenagers, worked in the bakery so they could earn some pocket money and help us at the same time. I made sure that they were treated as any other employees; they had a punch card and they made minimum wage. They worked ten hours per week on average, week-ends mostly, but on a regular basis. In the bakery, they served customers, and sometimes worked in the kitchen, preparing ham and cheese *croissants* and warming *Quiches Lorraine*. At any time, they could go from being a prep cook to being a waitress, cashier, or cleaning staff. Like everyone working there, they had to endure hearing the endless loop of French tunes sung by Edith Piaf, music that had to be played on stereo, over and over again, so that customers, walking in to buy a chocolate *croissant*, might fondly remember listening to "La Vie en Rose" at least once.

At Alain's urgent request once, when his office secretary left the company abruptly, Nathalie and I would alternate filling in for her. The secretary left at the worst time for a bakery business, three days before Christmas. With catering orders for bread, cakes and *Bûches de Noël*, pouring in by the dozens, we sorted piles of transactions printed on yellow paper and reviewed each of them by phone with the ordering customers.

On some occasions, the kids worked on the factory loading dock during the early morning shift, packing croissants, pastries, cakes and bread to be delivered around town. It was cold in the warehouse, particularly at Christmas time, and we had to work fast and pack everything carefully. Other times, Nathalie, who was old enough to have a driver's license, or I would drive the battered company van during the day and make a few deliveries to hotels or restaurants to help out in a pinch.

Even though the stores were open on Sundays, we tried each

week to keep that day as family time, going to Mass, driving to Galveston for a swim, playing mini-golf, enjoying the pool, cooking meals, and just spending time together. One Sunday, however, we got a 7:30 a.m. call from the dishwasher at Town and Country, who said the building was locked and no other workers had arrived. Even worse, there was a growing number of customers at the door. Alain and I woke up the kids, Armelle and Charles, who grumbled something about early Mass. "No Mass today," said Alain. We reached the store at record speed, unlocked the door and all jumped into jobs. Of the staff of six, that day, four were LeNôtres—Armelle at the cash register, Alain in the kitchen, Charles behind the counter, and me as a waitress. As I recall, all the customers went home happy.

The Macy's expansion was a problem from the start, mostly due to technicalities within the agreement. Our shop's employees would actually be Macy's employees, not ours, and they were just as likely to be assigned on any given day to some other station in the culinary department. There was no continuity for our customers and certainly no sanity for us. Every time we looked around, half the workers were people we'd never met, which also made proper training difficult.

Macy's had such high employee turnover that it proved impossible for anyone to truly know his or her job. On top of that, the three Macy's stores with our bakeries were open seven days a week but busy only on Saturday. And the store management insisted we keep our pastry showcases full at all times. The result: a level of pastry waste that destroyed our bottom line. When Macy's asked to terminate our contract, we were more than delighted to oblige.

Our success and failure as a family business came in waves. Yes, Houston was beginning its remarkable recovery from the recession, meaning that our problems would come from more specific sources. First, five years into the partnership, Albert Jamail passed away, leaving behind complications related to his succession. It was a sad thing for Houston to witness, since Jamail's was such a beloved and successful brand. Sales at the stores dropped. By the time a bank took over, the business was too far gone to save. We'd lost our single most successful store.

It wasn't long before our Sakowitz visibility, part of the LeNôtre adventure in America since the beginning, went away too. With five outlets down, what were we to do with our employees, we wondered? We were emotionally attached to these people, as they had supported us all the way through. We did not want to dismiss any of them. Instead, we diversified our operation into wholesale pastry baking, catering, and wedding cakes. We needed income. And the places we ended up finding it still make lots of people smile. How about Whataburger? How about Denny's? How about HEB and Kroger Signature? We could earn our stripes as a commercial baking operation by serving such iconic all-American brands.

Necessity may always be the mother of invention, but never more than when you need an income. While we continued to do high-profile catering and wedding cakes in and around Houston, it was unclear how we'd ever generate enough revenue to pay all our employees each week and still have something left over to pay ourselves. This was the mood and the mindset that produced opportunities in places we would least have expected them, and without a doubt generated the financial momentum Alain and I needed to move forward.

Sometimes, it all begins with having an open mind. As we were looking for a partner to join forces with us, we found an ad in the paper, written by a young Californian couple. They were smart, we thought, using a computer and having a diploma in chemistry. Their plan was to start a chocolate factory from scratch, roasting the cocoa beans in house in Houston. We were not enthusiastic about their idea, but we stayed in touch.

One day, providentially, they called us. Their chocolate factory had been up and running for some time, but now, they had made it into a cookie company that turned out mountains of gourmet butter cookies each month based on four recipes: oatmeal raisin, white chocolate-macadamia nuts, chocolate chunks and peanut butter. They had a large order to fill for Costco and all their employees, late in their wages, had resigned. They placed that desperate call, asking us if we could organize a team that very day to make their cookies at their tiny bakery. Of course, there's virtually nothing about baking that Alain could not organize. But within six months, the couple closed their business and vanished from Houston.

In the process, we did not make money by helping them, but we learned specifically how to make American gourmet frozen raw butter cookies by using a special "extruding" machine. But how to sell them? Providence again came to our rescue. We had been in touch with a mergers and acquisitions lawyer whom we hired to find capital. He never achieved this, but he introduced us to his brother-in-law who was a born salesman.

His brother-in-law was able to sell our American, gourmet, pure butter, with nothing artificial, cookies to the Texas institution Whataburger. Founded in Corpus Christi, it was at the time, family-owned and headquartered there. What they needed from us, of course, was not burgers and fries but cookies—and later blueberry muffins. Cookies we had. We sold them on the idea of carrying four flavors, with the dough frozen raw in little buckets for defrosting and scooping onto trays and ready to be baked four times a day in each of the company's then-three hundred restaurants.

At the time, the owners not only appreciated Alain and me being a family business but also our being based in Texas. They always worked hard to get every product from Texas that they could, even as they started to expand their stores into neighboring Louisiana, Florida, and Oklahoma, and they could definitely get great cookies in Texas now. We loved these cookies—they had replaced the bread and butter for our children. Even Papy (this is what Gaston's grandchildren called him) loved them and asked us for the recipe. He was eager to present something new, something Texan, to the French! But of course.

We would regularly bring home a bucket of dough and bake cookies in our oven as needed for dessert. Our children shared them with their classmates. Papy Gaston came a few times to Houston, once when our son Gaston celebrated his first communion at St. Cecilia Catholic Church, and the entire LeNôtre family came from Paris to spend a few days at our home. I was proud to receive them and made sure they were well treated. We did not have much money then, but we kept a house maid and Gaston came with cases of his Champagne, so it was a celebration. Of course I served them our American cookies.

There was a snag, eventually. Training of employees at Whataburger was uneven. That meant sometimes "closers" forgot to start thawing the cookie dough late at night in the coolers. In the morning, therefore, it was too hard to scoop. Alain met with the company's buyer (surely, it didn't hurt that we also took him and his family for a ten-day tour of Bordeaux, the Loire Valley and Paris) and worked out a solution.

Initially, Alain had the idea of buying a hamburger patty machine and using it to form ready to bake patties from cookie dough instead, but in the end the machine was too expensive for the volume of cookies. Eventually, with our client's approval we settled on using a "co-packer," a separate company, which had that type of equipment that could make and form the dough using our recipe and freeze it, in what resembled "hockey pucks."

We had more than a few giggles over that, but it also got Whataburger the cookies it needed for baking each day with consistency, without any of the old scooping nightmare. This being America, the co-packer was soon sold to a much larger national cookie company. Eventually the new owner started maneuvering to sell cookies directly to Whataburger and hired our salesman in the process.

We sued them and won, based on our contract prohibiting precisely that. We didn't get much money in the settlement. We did, however, manage to sell cookies to Whataburger, which by this time had about six hundred restaurants, for a few more years. We worked with Whataburger for fifteen years in all, until the chain decided to go with pre-baked cookies individually wrapped in cellophane. What a pity, we thought! Whataburger would never again serve our perfect freshly baked pure butter cookie, crispy on the outside and chewy on the inside that had been so unique to their brand.

Whataburger might have saved us in this country, keeping us around long enough to take the phone call from Denny's. Denny's had found us thanks to a four-line ad Alain had placed in a national wholesale bakery magazine. Another iconic all-American brand, Denny's liked to serve their own fresh-baked pies made daily and locally. They had their own plants on the East and West Coasts. In the great American middle, though, they were having problems getting fresh good pies delivered to each Denny's restaurant. They had twenty-two stores in the Houston area, and they wanted twelve types of pie—you do the math. Or rather, we did the math and figured out a system to bake the pies Denny's needed in our small factory off I-10 and deliver them to eleven stores one day and the other eleven the next. *Voilá*, fresh pies at Denny's made by LeNôtre chefs.

When you factor in the blueberry muffins for Whataburger, the HEB butter sugar cookies—provided raw on a stick, which the store baked and decorated according to the month's holiday, Christmas, Valentine's, St Patrick's Day or Easter—the Denny's pies, a line of nine French pastries for the newly obtained Kroger Signature account, the products for our Town & Country bakery café, plus catering and wedding cakes, we were getting cramped for space on I-10.

We hired a real estate broker to look around Houston for something bigger. He eventually hooked us up with another promising spot that was fully equipped with walk-in freezers and coolers. The brokers worked out the details, the closing was scheduled and then the two brokers went out to play a round of celebratory golf.

While they were busy on the links, destiny rang again. It was that Chinese real estate investor, the one who had bought our original plant building on I-45 from the two French banks. When Alain answered, the investor told him, "I'm ready to strike a deal with you. I'm ready to offer you the opportunity to lease the plant that you built on I-45."How ironic, we thought. We could get back to our own building!

Alain told the man it was more space than we needed, perhaps twice as much, and we'd already agreed to the right amount of space at the right price somewhere else. The closing, in fact, was for the very next day!

"What are you paying?" the investor said. He then offered to rent us the building for the same price. We negotiated a lease with an option to buy. By the time the two brokers finished their golf game, the new deal was done. Texans being Texans, they took the news in stride, shaking our hands and wishing us all the best. *Et voilá*. We were back to the beginning! Back in our building on I-45.

We had a huge space now and therefore felt compelled to use it. Like Houston itself, we had weathered the storm and emerged stronger than we ever imagined we could be. We were going to make money and start to pay ourselves and pay health insurance for the staff. And best of all, we had found our way home.

But not quite yet. The month we moved into our new headquarters, our catering chef and party planner left with our client list, putting an end to our catering business.

*Alain and I celebrate my first American degree,
in Psychology, at the University of Houston.*

CHAPTER 11

Educating Marie

> *The path to spiritual growth is a path of lifelong learning.*
>
> **M. SCOTT PECK**

Some people—knowing how involved I was with our business throughout that first decade or so in Houston, running shops and going on business trips to places like Walmart in Arkansas, Mary Kay cosmetics in Dallas, United Airlines in Chicago, or visiting with a franchise consultant and TV marketer in Philadelphia—are surprised to find out that I also went to school during those years. It simply seemed time to build my base of knowledge, which I had almost completely ignored in my youth, when so many things were confusing to me.

Returning to school later in life, I had a much easier time knowing exactly what I wanted to learn and committing myself to accomplishing it. Before this fifteen-year phase had ended, I had earned my bachelor's degree, two master's degrees and audited the classes for a third. Yes, all this meant time away from our business and away from my kids. But together we made it work somehow. My two teenage daughters, who knew the subject better, were helping me with algebra. They would say "Mom, don't ask why a+b = c, just take it as a given. There is no meaning to that." But my mind always tries to understand how things work and why, and I love to find out. A new world was opening to me, and like a child, I was wandering and wondering and living in a cocoon of higher education. Alain, in fact, cried when I first announced in 1986 that I would now be a student and would help less with the bakery. He soon recovered and seemed to enjoy my studies, even though they meant he had to shoulder more of the business himself.

I can't tell you how many hundreds of times I read to Alain from my textbooks, excited by something I hadn't known or hadn't thought about before, only for him to offer some brief commentary that set us to talking for hours. I like to joke that Alain learned as much from all my courses as I did, so we remained at the same level. We learned a lot, ultimately, together.

My education grew, I now understand, from my desire to do something more with my life than sell croissants, as much as I understood that we needed to sell plenty of them every day. That question led me into therapy for a brief time, and finally into a much longer and more meaningful encounter with what must have seemed learning for learning's sake. All I knew was that I felt a need to learn. This personal time was crucial to my mind, soul and inner peace. I needed to understand and also grow spiritually.

The therapy was suggested by my friend Lynn Lasher, who from our personal conversations recognized how much I was struggling with the purpose of my life. Indeed, so much had changed in the relatively brief time Alain and I had been married, going from having jobs within a stable international corporation in Paris to being involuntary entrepreneurs investing our own money in Houston, Texas. As time went by, and as the money we had kept dwindling even as we kept seeing some new light at the end of a tunnel, I found myself feeling lost.

I realized that this was where therapists could be helpful, so I went to see a therapist for maybe ten helpful visits. In our situation, I didn't feel comfortable spending the fortune required to see her indefinitely. Something about that New York picture of everybody in town seeing their therapist every week was not for me—the Woody Allen films, I had seen them all! So I decided I was not going to linger on a couch forever.

One especially meaningful piece of my own therapy puzzle was writing. My therapist essentially ordered me to start writing about my life. At first I thought that I couldn't remember anything at all, but this didn't hold up for very long. As I got started writing, by hand in those days, my life came back to me, eventually in huge torrents of stark emotion: my parents and their failings, the horrible war years of my earliest life, the hectic and unfulfilling abracadabra of stage and movie acting, all the traumas of dreaming of love and finding only sex. My recall seemed total on some days. I was crying and writing, crying and writing. Each week I would take some new batch of my memories to the therapist and with her help discover what they meant. And that was what we would talk about.

At one session she told me to get a thick pillow or better a punching bag, which I already had hanging in our living room for exercise, and strike it as hard as I could while thinking of my mother! She wanted to help me get rid of my anger. Another time, she told me to rent war movies and watch them with the sound turned up as loud as possible, as I thought about the war. That worked too. I was healing and, at the same time, I was discovering myself, perhaps the last person I ever expected to meet. It was a shock.

Another meaningful piece of my therapy puzzle was writing poetry. As a teenager I loved writing poetry. Often, I would lie alone on my bed, tears rolling down my cheeks, writing. I showed my poems to no one, of course. It was a way for me to express the fears, deceptions, misunderstandings, and traumas I had experienced. Later, in 1993, while I attended the University of Houston Creative Writing program, I took several courses in poetry, listening to my teachers and other classmates' own poems and their comments. I started to write poems again. It was a time I still cherish.

Looking back, my studies at the University of Houston

mirrored my own personal journey. I started in hospitality at the UH Hilton School, since that no doubt fed most directly into the business we were in. But the truth is, I wasn't fascinated by any of the courses offered, because I was doing these things at work every day. I moved from there to mass communications, another area that had held my interest off and on and was certainly one I'd more than dabbled in, beginning when the LeNôtre family was still the LeNôtre family.

I tried that route, radio and television specifically, thinking that perhaps Alain and I would someday create a TV cooking show school. But in the 1980s, before the Food Network and its many clones, this still seemed a strange idea. With this course, I also took an Introduction to Psychology which changed the entire picture of the world as I saw it then. My therapist had given me a push to try this, and as I amassed knowledge in the field, I finally settled on majoring in psychology.

With psychology I discovered a tool to understand the workings of the body and mind and the emotions and behavior that resulted from interactions. It was painful and enlightening at the same time. I became reacquainted with pain of the movie director abusing me as a teen-age actress that I had not felt consciously earlier. Instinctively, I had pushed the entire incident to the back of my brain pretending that nothing important or serious had happened. I was resilient, life goes on, and we need to forget. But forgive? At that time there was no space for that. There was hate, dismissiveness, and natural desire to get this guy far away from me! But worst of all, I hated myself.

Of course I blamed my mother first for everything. Later, I had to forgive her also. She did not know, I am sure. She had not considered the consequences, as she had no experience with men like this whatsoever, having been married immediately after finishing high school at eighteen. And her marriage was somewhat arranged. At those times, nice girls did not go out and party. To meet young women, a man had to be invited in the family and meet the parents first and make a good impression. My mother had several suitors but chose my father, the one she really liked.

There was a mutual attraction between the two of them, thank God; my mother married, and I am sure at the time she did not have a clue about how children were conceived or even about her own anatomy.

I had to forgive the movie director, also. Abusive men like that are everywhere. They are miserable, poor souls. What is society to do with them? There is no space in prisons. Unfortunately they are seldom punished, and the crimes against young girls and boys go on indefinitely.

I remember once my son Gaston, he must have been the same age I had been when I started acting, thirteen or fourteen years old. He was handsome, blond, and athletic. He had regular tennis lessons at Memorial High School with a private teacher. Sometimes in the afternoon he would walk by himself to the court, which was steps away from our house to practice and play with other boys. One afternoon he came back home from the tennis courts with an older man, tanned, in his mid-thirties, dressed in shorts and shirt, who asked us if he could take Gaston to the movies. My son was very enthusiastic with this prospect, but a thousand alarms went off in my head. I kept calm and thanked that man for his kind offer, but declined and made him understand that he should not see or invite Gaston again. The encounter was brief and to the point. Afterwards, I had a private talk with my son.

"You know, " I said, "this man might have some weird ideas in mind about you. He might want to seduce you."

"Really? "Gaston exclaimed, smiling innocently.

"Yes," I continued. "It happens all the time, older men with younger ones like you. What else do you think he had in mind when he invited you?"

Gaston looked at me flabbergasted.

"I would have never thought about that," he said.

Subsequently, I wanted to help others as much as my therapist and the study of psychology had helped me, particularly in dealing with the kinds of issues that have always haunted my life. I took a course in human sexuality, one of those general survey courses in an auditorium with about five-hundred other students, watching the diverse details from transsexual transformation to intercourse techniques for seniors.

I read so many relevant books, most on personal development, like *The Road Less Traveled*, and I was always excited to race home to share what I'd learned with Alain. He would be back from a draining day at the plant or in some stores, but he seemed very enthusiastic about all we discussed. Maybe his name should have been beside mine on the degree in psychology I earned in 1989.

The journals I'd been writing ever since therapy inspired my next step. I had planned to become a therapist, which would have required a Ph.D., and I had a difficult time convincing my advisers to let me enter that program. My GRE scores were not impressive because of my weakness in math and the fact that English was my third language. I didn't see why those GRE scores mattered so much for the type of help I wanted to give to people, but I wouldn't be the first or the last grad student to face a wall she couldn't climb without knowing why the wall was there in the first place.

I was encouraged to set my sights lower, perhaps on education counseling or on social work, which would require "only" a master's degree. And I was accepted into the School of Social Work, but I never started as I was much too busy writing a book, *White Lamb*.

Over the next few years, *White Lamb* would take many forms: 100% nonfiction, 100% fiction, and just about everything in between. I was writing in French, since that's the language that still came most easily to me. I decided to write the book in English next, since English was the language of my newfound life. And after all, everything was possible in America, I thought.

I hired a bilingual American writer and she and I had the best time, as I was seeing my story in a different light, and through a different perspective. Writing down all the things that had happened to me when I was fourteen, I saw that they looked much less terrible, less depressing on paper. Working with her on my story was a little like having a best friend, as she came to be intimate with all my frailties. I remember that when I told a friend I was rewriting *White Lamb* in English, he laughed and said, "Can you imagine Tolstoy rewriting *War and Peace* in English?" It didn't discourage me, and I was not Tolstoy, either.

Besides writing, I was also interested in medicine and health. After all, a million years ago, being a doctor had been one of my earliest dreams. As the ancient Greeks used to say and practice, a healthy mind resides in a healthy body. Now, rather than simply dream, I had found a path into the field. I was accepted into the School of Public Health, the UT Health Science Center in downtown Houston, to pursue studies in "health promotion and health education." Essentially, I wanted to capitalize on all that I had learned in the field of Psychology and Health. My first paper was on teen suicide, a subject I knew first-hand. My advisor gave me excellent grades and comments, though she disliked the subject, feeling it was too controversial.

When I suggested I write my master's thesis on abortion, a battleground which intrigued me because of its ethical components, my advisor recognized just what a complicated and even more controversial subject this would be. Instead, she led me toward her own chosen subject: adolescents, especially girls. In particular, she suggested I look at how teen girls who suffer from hopelessness, depression, or attempts at suicide are supported during times of crisis. I was interested, of course. Within a year and a half, I earned a master's in public health with a thesis titled "Perception of Social Support, Life Events, and Depression/ Hopelessness in Children and Adolescents." Still, my advisor shook her head, "You did it too quickly," she said.

For me it was not too quick, as through it all I'd become interested—passionate might be a better word—in the ways that religious faith, the belief that there is a God who cares about us, impacts our mental and physical health. Specifically, I wanted to do research on the relationship between prayer and healing. Dealing with the issues before me, in my life as well as in class after class, project after project, it simply struck me how much more likely you are to be happy, perform well, or stay healthy, when you conduct yourself in the light of a loving God. I was clinical about it; this was no mere emotional thing for me. But it seemed to be true, and I longed to know more, read more, and experience more.

There was some talk, early on, about establishing this as a specific course of study at the School of Public Health, by a professor who was an atheist himself but whose father had been a minister. This professor had nightmares about the devil constantly, he told me, and he wanted to exorcise himself. He also wanted to find God and his grace. We talked about designing a "spirituality and health" curriculum, with me essentially as the guinea pig working toward my Ph.D. in that subject.

We had meetings with fellows from nursing schools, whose research had shown again and again that spirituality did matter to one's health and overall well-being. I still remember a research paper I read about "laughing and being good to others and the correlation of one's health." I was enthralled with the prospect of this research, as I was convinced that all these things had value and were relevant in people's lives.

But my former advisor intervened and vehemently opposed my participation in the program, pointing to my weak background in all things statistical. And my would-be doctoral professor and advisor backed away. He proposed instead that I study to take another GRE exam for my participation in these doctoral studies, which I refused. I knew I was not gifted for that, and I had had enough statistics and biometrics anyway. That ended our plan. The program we'd talked about for several weeks was abandoned. Getting a doctorate from the School of Public Health was not meant to be.

I was disheartened, of course. But, at that crucial moment, I remembered my book. That became my whole purpose, which led me to the Masters in English and Creative Writing Program at the University of Houston. The creative writing program at UH was doing wonderful things in those days, and it was recognized as the number two program in the country after Iowa. Distinguished writers and poets, like Richard Howard, Adam Zagajewski, and Edward Albee, excited me, along with the other respected novelists and poets already "in residence" in our department. My daughter Nathalie was especially proud of me for being accepted there for a graduate degree, as she herself first contemplated the idea of studying literature instead of medicine.

Best of all, I started writing again in a more supportive setting. Writing is by nature quite lonely, but it feels better if you're writing within a group, sharing and supporting each other's efforts, and offering comments that can make all the difference. Yes, of course, I had to learn to take criticism without falling apart.

"Not enough drama," one professor said. "Not enough action," said another. My manuscript was often scratched on the sides in red with the word "Awkward."

"Why don't you write in your mother tongue!" my advisor burst out in one of our rare meetings—as she was busy writing her own novel which was published soon afterwards.

But the more I wrote my story anew, using the skills I was developing, the more my professors and my fellow classmates seemed to like it. I earned my second master's degree from UH in creative writing. I sent my manuscript to all the usual suspects in New York, one after another for a period of a year. All I got were rejection slips. At one point I was so desperate, I sent an email to my adviser asking her to help me find a publisher. She had an obligation, I asserted, to follow through and help me, to do something. No answer came back.

So, there I was, thinking that I had to let go of my book, *White Lamb,* and that it was finally time for theology to take over my life. My decision was born of my awareness that I knew so little about God, and religion, which seemed extraordinarily significant for so many people. I had a few notions about it, growing up Orthodox in Greece, and I'd learned about Catholicism from Alain's ardent faith. But why, how, and when were these belief systems formed? Why have they had such an impact on us? Why the liturgy? And why the Eucharist? All that was *terra incognita* to me.

I was soon accepted into the master's program in theological studies at St. Mary's Seminary at the University of St. Thomas in Houston, a program that was about 90% men headed for the priesthood and 10% lay people, interested in pursuing doctoral studies or learning more about their faith. Still, there was the issue of time available to me, since I'd never stopped working beside Alain in our business. Because I was fascinated with theology for my own faith development, I decided to skip writing all the papers the program demanded for another master's and simply audit the courses. I would never become a theologian, I thought, so why seek a third master's degree? I realized getting degrees and learning had become an addiction.

In the end, the decision was, well, a godsend. I would settle for nothing less than an A on any school work I did, which produced a lot of stress. Even seeing a "B" on a paper caused me to develop ulcers in and around my mouth, and obviously this didn't strike me as healthy. Auditing the coursework meant that I could give myself permission to simply enrich my life. Without really planning to, I ended up studying the impact of faith on a human life. And the life I was studying eventually became my own.

We worked our way through the Old Testament stories of the Jewish people, and through the New Testament assertion of Jesus' unique and transformative role in what I came to see as salvation history. There was so much information to take in— so much good and sometimes not so good, since, yes, that was covered too.

We learned about the Historical Jesus, and the ramifications of his birth and resurrection, the Gospels and the Pauline writings and the truth about which of them were genuine or not, etc. We studied arguments and perspectives concerning the Jewish/ Catholic relations, the papacy within the Catholic Church, and even Church building design and architecture. As I was eagerly participating in class, Father Anderson, my most beloved professor, kept asking me to write papers on each subject. I reminded him that I was only an auditing student, yet he kept asking.

I read many books about the early Christian times, and other manuscripts, even in French, which recounted the lives of the religious in the Renaissance period. I spent days and weeks in the St. Mary's Seminary library reading everything that I was assigned. My favorite book was by Cardinal Joseph Kasper, *The God of Jesus Christ,* which he closes by saying, "We know nothing about God. God is unfathomable."

When I finished the program in 2002, I had not resolved all my questions about Christian theology in the least. Certainly, some of my questions were answered during my studies, but new questions endlessly emerged.

Nevertheless, I realized that the God question could be subjective, and religion in general is often tied to political and social systems. Since the beginning of our human history we have the need to explain the awesome thing that is our vast universe, which contains roughly 100 billion galaxies, each galaxy, our Milky Way for instance, may contain 400 billion stars. For me, God is that life force which created the world out of unstructured meaningless chaos and made it into a sparkling myriad of stars and galaxies. I also believe that God is the life force inside me that sustains me and connects me with the universe. As long as I breathe in and breathe out, I am able to feel that connection.

We do not think about this every day, and I suppose ancient people had more time and leisure to wonder and be afraid of all that they did not know about the cosmos. Today, the great mystery of the when, how, and why of life's origins remains, even though we know its fundamental prerequisites. Theology and astrophysics are matters that I am passionate about, and I keep searching to learn and understand. "There is no such thing as too much learning, when it comes to education," wrote acclaimed Chef Daniel Boulud in his *Letter to a Young Chef.*

The truth is that being so involved professionally in the education field with our Culinary Institute, I find my needs fulfilled and my identity crystallized. Because working for something that matters to me, I feel my life becomes a lighthouse. Sharing knowledge with others, helping them grow professionally and spiritually, I feel I am accomplishing a higher purpose. Closing another circle in my life, my own studies at UH, UTSPH and St. Thomas helped me to understand the meaning of the education and opportunity the Culinary Institute provides.

*Gaston LeNotre with his infant grandson Gaston Jr.
celebrates the opening of the LeNôtre Boutique on I-45 in
Houston, 1983.*

CHAPTER 12

Struggling To Say Good-Bye

To love someone is to see him as God intended him.

DOSTOEVSKY

Even as our business life in Houston started to become successful at long last, Alain LeNôtre and I always made a point of knowing where our children were. Sometimes that was easy, as when all five of them—Nathalie and Armelle, Cecile and Charles, and our young son Gaston—were living at our house in Memorial.

With Alain's kids, the idea at the start was that they'd spend a year with us and a year with their mother in Paris. It was like those alternating weekends so typical of American divorces, except with a very large ocean in between. Eventually, this plan gave way to Alain's son living with his father and Alain's daughter living with her mother, a reasonable approach to the difficult teenage years. This plan worked. Both of Alain's children ended up attending respected hotel-restaurant management schools—Cécile in Lausanne, Switzerland, eventually becoming an executive with Club Med after spending eight years at Disneyland Paris, and Charles at the Lyon Bocuse School. He eventually opted out of chef whites for a life in finance and administration for an upscale casino-hotel-restaurant near Lyon.

We had a similar arrangement with my two daughters. They'd spend a year with us and a year in Provence with their father. As part of the three or four or five children living in our home at any one time, with a nanny to help out during the long hours Alain and I were working, my daughters came to prosper in their own ways.

My first, Nathalie earned her MD from the University of Texas Medical Branch in Galveston. She pursued an Internal Medicine Residency at Georgetown University and completed a fellowship in Infectious Diseases at Harvard and Cornell University. She now works in private practice. My second daughter, Armelle, earned a Ph.D. in molecular biology at Princeton and works in informal science education and policy in New Mexico.

As for our youngest, Gaston, he took after his father far more than his grandfather when it came to spirituality. Before deciding which high school to attend, he actually asked us for an hour to meditate. And after four sterling years at Strake Jesuit in Houston, he completed his coursework in philosophy at the University of St. Thomas while also pursuing a three-year pre-seminary program. He then travelled to Rome where he decided that his vocation would be fatherhood. Today, he is busy completing his doctoral dissertation in Philosophy at Catholic University of America in Washington, D.C., and is also working as compliance manager at our Culinary Institute.

But I suppose we acted all along as Alain's parents did, working passionately and continuously for their business, letting the kids grow up almost by themselves. That is the other side of the coin, I suppose. History repeats itself unless one is strong enough to change its course.

Sometimes, early on, life is all about living. We grow up, get married, have children, and build a business. But eventually, when we live long enough, life gets to be a lot about dying. A certain component of our life in Houston has been struggling to say goodbye.

The first farewell was to my first husband, Alain Casau. As the years had passed, and certainly as I came to understand myself better, I came to understand him better too. Like so many men, Alain Casau had had issues with his father. Although he had never complained or showed sadness, it was difficult to have a father who was a wealthy man and couldn't spare ten dollars to help his son. The result was a grown man who was intelligent, hard-working and successful, a man who always loved our two daughters, his dogs, and science, but who seemed unhappy with himself while we lived together.

I was deeply saddened when I heard of Alain's Casau death to lung cancer. He was such a quiet and gentle person, and far too young to leave this world. However, I don't know whether he saw it that way. What I do know is that before he died at home with his third wife and their son at his side, he called me home and told me how special I was in his life, and how he had missed my presence and smile. A week later I received a little postcard which said that he was leaving this world in peace and with great hopes that we might meet again soon somewhere beyond the sky!

I am still trying to locate that postcard to show my daughters and also to decipher the meaning of it. I had thought wrongly that he had been a serious atheist all the time I knew him.

The death, also to cancer, of Alain LeNôtre's first wife Catherine put us in the situation of both being widowed. Like my first husband, Catherine had remained as close as she could to her children. Not only did she never have a non-LeNôtre husband, as she never remarried, but she never had a non-LeNôtre job. She was still running the flagship store in Auteuil all those years after the divorce and later on she was responsible in forming all new LeNôtre boutique employees.

For his part, Alain had forgiven her. We always visited her when we were in Paris, and she always received both of us warmly, offering us chocolates or *macarons*. On one of those visits, while the three of us had dinner and sipped wine at Jules Verne, the restaurant on the second floor of the Eiffel Tower, the light banter touched on our two marriages to Alain.

"Can you believe it, Catherine?" Alain said. "Marie and I have been married for twenty-five years."

"Oh no," she responded with a cheerful smile. "I never could have lasted that long!"

When cancer took her life, Catherine's closest family and friends were shocked. They had never known she was so ill. She had that kind of pride . Her funeral was held in the same church where she and Alain had been married.

Catherine's passing was a heavy loss to Cecile and Charles who adored their mother and also had not realized how ill she was. But like her, they would not show how it affected them. How fleeting life is, I thought, so year after year we make sure to spend meaningful family time with all our children and their families gathered for the holidays in the US or in France.

At the time of Catherine's death, Alain and I, who had both been active in a Francophone Catholic Parish at St. Basil's Chapel, made a pilgrimage to the Holy Land. This trip to Israel, with a French-speaking Catholic group from France, Belgium, Switzerland, Cameroon, and Mauritius, was unforgettable, even to us who had visited so many places. We were immersed in the limpid waters of Jordan River, wearing long white robes, and we swam afterwards in the same holy waters with which John had baptized Jesus.

We renewed our wedding vows in Cana, where Jesus' attendance at a wedding feast had led to his first public miracle. Jerusalem reminded me so much of Athens: the trees, the hills, the dazzling sun. The energy of the entire landscape emanates a palpable emotion. Being there felt like living in history's most extraordinary times.

And finally, after all the joy and suffering we had been through with him and because of him, it was time to say goodbye to Gaston, the father. The great chef Gaston LeNôtre's final years were shaped by the fact that after twenty years of separation from Colette—who had been such an equal partner in creating and maintaining the LeNôtre empire—he had resigned himself to divorce and married his much younger mistress of twenty-five years.

Gaston and his new wife were living primarily at his hunting ranch in Sologne, quite possibly the place he had been happiest of all with Colette. His financial power was diminished when the proceeds of the sale of their business were split between Colette and him following their separation. Gone were the high-profile, big budget hunts for top-dollar catering clients of the LeNôtre enterprise, the extravagant food and wine served. Even without that excitement, though, he was enormously attached to his land. He had turned it into a visual enchantment with three ponds and made it a kind of wonderland filled with wild animals he lured onto the property by setting out grain.

After the sale of all LeNôtre culinary enterprises, Gaston had remained a highly visible public figure in the company, especially in France. He stayed on as Chairman of the Board, a figurehead position he never failed to enjoy. He had no hand in decision-making, but he was front and center for public relations. The truth is, however, Gaston had far less to do during his golden years than his ambition and energy demanded.

He considered many business opportunities, but, eventually, he settled on purchasing Château Fesles, a winery with vineyards in the beautiful Loire Valley Coteaux du Layon. He had to remodel the *château* and called on Colette, rather than his second wife, to advise him in interior decorating. Gaston had many big ideas for developing and improving the wines from his chateau, which included whites, reds, roses and a dessert wine, a Bonnezeaux appellation that resembled *Sauternes*. He invested big piles of his money to achieve his dream, updating and upgrading the ancient chateau cellar to showcase the towering stainless steel vats found in upstart winemaking places like California. Yet he soon realized that he was not growing enough grapes for the scale of his oversized cellar equipment, so instead of buying grapes from others, he bought two more wine properties, including La Roulerie, a *château* from the Renaissance.

Still, every year the business lost money, a process helped along by his tendency to take advice from anyone who used flattery to try to sell him something. Gaston finally sold his Loire

Valley holdings after a decade or so, the sale bringing in enough to cover the debts his wine venture had amassed.

When Gaston was diagnosed with his cancer, and after he had undergone his ordeal of chemotherapy and surgery, Sylvie and Annie had been taking turns for several weeks at Gaston's bedside. But the day of Christmas 2008, Colette called and warned us—she feared these were his final days. Though Gaston had not been a practicing Catholic in many decades, he had asked us to pray that he might leave the hospital and return to die at home, in Sologne. And so we had, and Gaston was now home.

We flew without any delay to Paris to visit him and were surprised at how frail the man felt when we embraced him. Stroking the back of Gaston's head, Alain noticed how thin and silky the remaining hair had become—soft as a baby's first hair, he realized.

"You've been too far, too long, my son," Gaston mumbled, as Alain kissed his hand.

Now it was just before New Year's Eve, the dead of winter in the French countryside. Gaston had endured many surgeries, but none had stopped the spread of cancer. At last he was home at his hunting lodge in Sologne with his two Braque pointer dogs at his side and settled into a bed set up in the salon, next to the fireplace with a view of his land and frozen ponds through wide picture windows. The grass of so many remembered summers lay deep beneath the snow.

As we watched him from morning to evening the old patriarch declined a bit more each day, with his doctor giving him morphine for the pain. We had plane reservations back to Houston but, fearing the end was near, decided to stay on, and accompany him till the end. We would take our breakfast every morning, gazing on the still lake and the ducks and watching Gaston, who was lying on a hospital stretcher next to us. Afterwards, Alain would read to him, praying for a miracle.

Alain managed to convince Gaston's new wife to let him call a village priest to administer the last sacraments. We knew the end was coming. The ancient priest, long retired from the village parish, was of the old-fashioned, gentle-speaking variety.

"I won't be very long; everything will be fine, do not worry," he reassured Gaston's wife, who was not in the least religious and withdrew from the salon. He gave the old man the last rites, and we sat in silence. Then, breaking the quiet, the priest asked him. "Mr. LeNôtre, are you happy now?"

We almost stepped in, to explain that Gaston had long stopped speaking to anyone, that he had laid inert in bed only listening a little as Alain read to him from the daily *Figaro* newspaper.

"*Oui*," whispered Gaston LeNôtre. "*Je suis heureux.*"

As the priest put on his thick coat and beret and walked out to his tiny car for the drive through the snow, we told him those were Gaston's only words in two weeks.

The old priest smiled. "They all do that to me," he said softly.

There was so much time to think of the long and painful journey Alain and I had endured because of his father. But, the truth was, all that had been washed away as gently and inevitably as the sea washes away the shore. Gaston was dying and we pitied him immensely. Alain constantly had tears in his eyes and made sure that his father knew that he was next to him and that he loved him and had forgiven him. He was a good man in his heart and had done his best, we knew. He had suffered, and I am sure he had realized his shortcomings and misdemeanors. We did not want him to die.

Gaston's passing away two days later, on January 8, 2009, launched a series of public and private events that made it seem as though the man had been a prime minister or sports celebrity. As a great French chef, of course, he was a bit of both. On television, newspapers and magazines over the world, Gaston was praised by all—including president Sarkozy and *The New York Times*—as equaled only by Escoffier, the culinary icon who modernized French cuisine and revolutionized the way people feast, wine, and dine. "Mr. LeNôtre was the exacting patriarch of French *pâtisserie*," The *Times* obituary said. "He rejuvenated pastry making in the early 1960s and then created a worldwide group of 60 boutiques in 12 countries, which can cater to every whim, from truffled *pâté* for 25,000 guests, to a banquet for the queen of England, all with French flair, service and decorum."

The company that still owned his image staged a dazzling funeral mass (without the casket) at the Church of La Madeleine off the Place de La Concorde in Paris with a thousand attendants. Alain read the Psalm, and Gaston's grandson, our Gaston, was the altar boy. Many famous chefs were in church that day— Bocuse, Troisgros, Guerard, and dozens of others—gathered to hear a series of speeches, including one by popular actor and humorist Henri Tisot, whose father had been a pastry chef and painter in Provence.

Alain saved his speech for the second religious service, held the next day at La Couture Basilica and Cemetery in Bernay, where Alain's grandparents, Eleonore and Gaston, were buried. There were many in attendance, mostly LeNôtre employees but also family members and friends from Normandy, underlining the simple fact that Gaston had gone to Paris to work but now had come home to rest.

It was particularly cold and rainy that day, even for January. But that didn't keep an honor guard of 60 chefs wearing their white jackets and high toques blanches from lining the casket's brief passage from church to churchyard grave, where Gaston had earlier bought two plots alongside his parents for himself and his brother Marcel.

In that quiet churchyard deep in Normandy, Gaston was buried beside the two chefs who gave him life. Less than two years later, his beloved younger brother Marcel took the place beside him.

Students throwing hats in the Cafe after Graduation

CHAPTER 13

Taste & See

Wherever you go, go with all your heart.
CONFUCIUS

In one of this world's nicest twists, my tireless pursuit of education led me and Alain toward offering education ourselves. We were back in our original 28,000-square-feet building, designed and equipped initially to train all the employees for what was supposed to be 20 LeNôtre boutiques all over the Sunbelt. Half of that plant, mostly on the second floor, was still unoccupied since the wholesale bakery production was located on the first floor. As when Alain opened École LeNôtre in Plaisir, and when we first planned to duplicate it in Houston in 1984 without success, everything within us yearned again to share our passion, the LeNôtre pastry and culinary knowledge.

With the assistance of two marketing students from the University of Houston looking for a case study towards their degree, we surveyed the market so that we could offer a hands-on high quality training education in the US. The survey findings were encouraging. We invited Alain's cousin Patrick, a two-star Michelin chef in both pastry and cooking, to move here from

Paris, set up the curriculum, and teach the first courses. We opened in 1998 under the name Culinary Institute Alain and Marie LeNôtre.

On the one hand, this was not a perfect system, since Patrick could teach only in French. But we solved that problem by enrolling the wives of French astronauts in training at NASA at that time! They were bilingual, interested in French cuisine and pastry, and as they translated, they participated in the class, and earned certificates for themselves as their compensation. It suited everyone.

A stark reality check was born of our introduction to the American system of permits and eventual accreditations, subjects to which I had to devote every ounce of the scholarly research skill I'd developed. It was, in short, a tangled nightmare that took years. Within a week of getting our permits from the Texas Workforce Commission and starting to teach students, veteran *Houston Chronicle* food editor, Ann Criswell came in to interview us and write a story. The result was a two-page spread with photographs of students trying out new skills in our kitchen labs. A few more students trickled in after that, but it was slow.

One of our biggest challenges was understanding the very different way Americans approached culinary training—any career training, in fact—from the way people in France always did. There, the culinary career was a form of vocational-technical training, and people paid to get the skills that would help them land a good job in their field. In America, as we learned from mother after mother sitting with her son or daughter, people paid to get a degree in something. A diploma in cooking or baking wasn't enough, we soon realized; we had to develop and award an associate degree in the field. And we did so in 2006, developing three Associate Degrees, in Culinary Arts, Pastry Arts and Hospitality and in Restaurant Management.

To qualify, first, it took two years for me to execute the tedious administrative work required for us to be accredited by a national accreditation institution. And since we also realized that many of our students needed the same financial aid that their peers in colleges and universities relied upon—Pell grants and loans from the federal government—it took me another two years to comply with the administrative credentials that would earn us Title IV accreditation as an educational institution from the Federal Department of Education.

Then we could develop a curriculum for an associate's degree. In the end, it was all this work that I never could have done without my own adventures in higher education that allowed our Culinary Institute to grow to be what it is now: a 350-student institution where passion, dedication, hard work, and camaraderie merge together.

In the beginning of our Culinary Institute, very few students enrolled. We were not able to advertise, and the money was eroding fast as we needed to pay for chefs, employees and equipment to build and expand our classrooms.

I remember that Alain and I were doing all the jobs. At one point I was the business manager, paying the bills and writing the checks for our expenses. We were losing money. And I had calculated that if we reached fifty students we would break even and be able to keep the school alive. It happened, of course, but to me it felt unbearably long. I meditated for more students, and eventually I was visualizing all the classrooms full of students, and it happened. It really did. When we had reached 350 students, our laboratories were filled with white uniformed students, religiously listening to their chef and tending the oven, the knives and the skillets. I was in heaven, walking by the classes, saying *bonjour* to the students who would answer back with happy smiles.

Also at the very start, we inaugurated the Taste and See lunches, an innovation not included in most culinary arts programs. Students from their different labs at the end of class presented their prepared food and pastries in the student dining room. These presentations happened three times a day at the end of each shift. If you were a guest visiting at meal time, you could see several six-foot tables filled with quite elaborate dishes, pastries, and breads. Students would line up ceremoniously, and each class presented its dish—name, ingredients and techniques used. At the end of the presentation, guests and students filled their plates and tasted everything, commenting at each bite.

It was amazing to listen as they discussed the particularities of each dish. Eventually, pastry students enrolled in savory cuisine and cuisine students asked to enroll in pastry. And they were allowed to take home food and pastries for a modest sum of three or five dollars, which went directly into the scholarship fund. Not only our students, but the chefs, the management staff, the cleaning crews and prospective students and their guests, participate daily. Our tasting is a communion with food.

We learned so much as we moved through those first years—especially evolving from a program based on diplomas to become one built around associate degrees. We understood, however, that we needed to recruit and serve four different target audiences. The one we knew best, of course, was what we call career seekers: mostly young people, who were looking to start a career in cuisine with appropriate training. There were also more and more career changers, somewhat less young people tired of whatever corporate existence they had and wishing to "express themselves" more fully in the kitchen. There were also career enhancers; these were professional cooks, chefs or managers who'd already enjoyed some success in the field but who wanted to fill an empty spot when it came to formal training and a rich résumé.

Finally, there were the culinary enthusiasts. After decades of treating chefs as cooks and cooks as mere laborers, everyday Americans fell in love with everything about chefs. This meant that hundreds and even thousands of prospective students who'd never seek a job in a restaurant would indeed love to take our courses, fast-track and stand-alone lessons in areas that interested them. We saw these people out there from the beginning.

What we didn't see in the beginning were all the foreign students we'd eventually attract. It required the growth of the Internet to accomplish this, so that students could learn more about our programs without calling to ask or waiting for a flyer to arrive in the mail. Students from as far away as Latin America and Southeast Asia would eventually make up a good percentage of our class roster, sometimes staying on to cook in America and other times returning home to practice their newly developed skills. I check with them often on Facebook, exchanging pictures of their dishes, announcing an engagement or a new birth in their family.

What I recognized early on that fascinated me most—and what convinced me we were doing something worthwhile—was the way all students became equals when they arrived at LeNôtre in the morning, afternoon or evening for class. Let's face it: they weren't equals on a socio-economic level. Some pulled into our parking lot in a Mercedes, or BMW, or even a Bentley, some straggled in driving rusted-out cars on their last legs, and still others walked or took the bus. They came to us with different levels of previous education, and they belonged to just about every conceivable ethnic group.

Once they were inside and changed into their white student uniforms, however, every difference seemed to disappear—age, gender, race. They were all suddenly working side by side in the same classroom to master the same culinary building blocks. I was deeply impressed by this, by the way they usually interacted and tried to help each other. It still makes me believe in what we're doing.

Interestingly, the one inequality we could never erase was the speed at which students were able to learn. There are, without fail in any group, faster learners and slower learners. And since they were all in the same classroom together, we addressed this by keeping classes really small—no more than twelve students— allowing our instructors to supply plenty of individual attention.

Some of our finest efforts of the past few years have focused on supplying an even more practical, real-world element to the high-quality training given by our instructors in class, all with more than ten years of chef experience. To that end, we institut- ed a mandatory "practicum" that sends our students for graded ten-week assignments at local hotels, restaurants, catering com- panies, and country clubs. We've seen this make a noticeable change in how ready our students are for the real working experience. They are learning exactly how to work in a professional setting where time is always of the essence, where the chef always has to be obeyed, and where the scallops can never be allowed to burn.

Furthermore, we have formed a student exchange partnership with the French school of Notre Dame du Roc in the province of Vendée on the Atlantic Coast. Each year we select a group of eight to fourteen students from our honor society to do their two months' practicum there, as well as upscale restaurants in Paris and Corsica. The joy and anticipation of the students planning their externship in France is a pleasure to witness. This exchange student program adds a great cultural dimension to our students' education. Of course, the French students love visiting Houston, as we put them up at friends' homes, often spectacular River Oaks mansions or charming Heights villas.

Our students have had the privilege to work in such places as the River Oaks Country Club under Chef Charles Carroll, or at Shade and Canopy restaurants under Chef Claire Smith, or Granduca Hotel. Our alumni are very much involved in our ongoing project, welcoming the students and inviting them to great Texas barbeques, baseball matches, or Galveston beach fun. I wish I had these kind of nurturing opportunities when I was studying back in Greece!

In addition to externships of this kind, we've also managed to create an opportunity for some of our most qualified students right inside Culinary Institute LeNôtre. During the school renovation that gave us our Crump amphitheater, we added the full-service restaurant named Kris Bistro, decorated lavishly by Jane-Page Crump. The artwork displayed is selected by international gallerist Elina Htun, who supports talented local artists. Twenty percent of these sales goes to our scholarship fund. We named the restaurant after Executive Chef Kris Jakob, who is our vice-president and director of education and also the mentor of the Bistro. Kris jokes that we only named it after him so he could never quit. This is true and it is not. We value Chef

Kris: his teaching style, his knowledge, his down-to-earth but also innovative methods and recipes, his graciousness. He has become a part of our school's dynamic and culture, and Kris Bistro is the proof. And since the opening, Chef Justin Santellana, a LeNôtre graduate, cooks and runs the kitchen smoothly and stylishly along with other graduates under him. This is another thing that I am proud of.

Over the years, we've learned that one size does not fit all when it comes to culinary education. In other words, the program that helps this student advance toward his or her goals is not necessarily going to help that one. As a result, we are now a Junior University, offering four different culinary diplomas options and three different associate degree versions with an additional three elective courses. We believe our students need to have as many options as possible. Helping this along are several new courses we've created in response to perceived needs.

Since 2014, wine, for instance, is now part of every student's curriculum. Seeing the explosion of interest in this country—and the dramatic improvement in wines made in California, Washington, Oregon and, yes, Texas—we knew we couldn't send forth students who had no clue about wine. There is a mandatory Wine Fundamentals class in all the associate-degree programs, plus two additional electives called LeNôtre Sommelier I and LeNôtre Sommelier II. The same kind of thing happens with our hotel management electives, and restaurant management electives, since we see more and more of our students finding opportunities in hotel kitchens and then hoping to rise into management. The days of chefs having no idea how the business is doing on a profit-and-loss statement and marketing are, we believe, over.

The heady mix of steady hard work and sometime celebrity in our world was brought into the spotlight in the summer of 2012, while we were enjoying our annual vacation on the isle of Corsica. I was checking my email, as we both do every day to keep up with things in Houston, and I noticed an email from legendary chef

Daniel Boulud. We'd met Daniel a few years earlier, when Alain and I had participated in a New York City fundraiser for Meals on Wheels.

In this email, he was asking if our school would donate a dozen students to work an event in Houston to benefit the US Bocuse d'Or, the international chef competition to which the United States always sends an entry. They were all hoping to raise money at a private event, featuring Daniel, Thomas Keller of French Laundry fame and Paul Bocuse's son Jerome, at the splendid River Oaks home of Deana and Larry Blackburn. I was amazed to see this email and responded with no delay.

"Of course," I said. "Our school is honored to be part of this event and will make one dozen students available for Chef to use in any capacity."

Over a series of emails, I told Daniel how much our students would enjoy a visit by him to our school—and how excited they'd be to purchase signed copies of his cookbooks. Additionally, we would make our entire campus available to Chef Boulud and his team for anything they might need: tools, kitchen space, etc., to facilitate the fundraising effort. Daniel Boulud responded, thanking me generously.

After a couple of days, though, an idea came to me. What if I asked Daniel if he could present me with the National Medal of Merit that President Sarkozy had awarded me in May of that year? This magnificent blue medal was sitting in my drawer waiting for something exciting to happen. And so I prayed first, then wrote an email asking Daniel that big favor, suggesting that after the medal awarding ceremony he might consider having a book signing on our campus.

I waited and fretted for a very long weekend before I got an affirmative answer from Chef. He even added that he would check on Chef Keller, who might be interested as well in visiting and having a book signing at the school. Needless to say, on September 28, all three chefs visited the school. Before long, Daniel was not only coming for a visit, but he was ceremonially presenting me with the award and, best of all, he was bringing

Keller and Bocuse along to share the fun.

In reality, the chefs had a lot to do in Houston and not much time to do it. You can imagine how pleased I was that all three came to our school, made it through all ten of our packed classrooms, signed books, shook hands with every student, and posed for photos with upwards of three hundred of our students before finally submitting to a meet-and-greet reception with a selected list of our VIPs. Each chef gave a speech to this crowd: Boulud's incorporated the presentation of my award in his speech; Bocuse's evoked the decades of friendship between his legendary father and Alain's; while Thomas Keller's speech explained how we never succeed alone but we always need a team, as encouragement to the students to go on with their dream and make things happen for themselves.

We like to think Gaston was smiling down on us that evening from someplace very peaceful and very happy. He could witness from above the success of his son and the continuation of his legacy in our own Culinary Institute LeNôtre that he never had a chance to visit.

In short, the famous chefs had a blast, visiting what they called the only French culinary university in the United States. And, at the Blackburns' fundraising dinner, they gave those twelve students the thrill of a culinary lifetime. Even better, Boulud and Keller ended up hiring three of them each. It was an event to remember. Their photos hang on the schools walls now. And we've also named three of our laboratories after them: Daniel Boulud, Thomas Keller and Jerome Bocuse.

Jane Page Crump with Dennis Steger, the 2114 and 2013
Gaston LeNôtre Scholarship Ambassador recipients

CHAPTER 14

My Very Best Friends

> *Whether or not we become blessed by grace is a matter of our choice. Essentially grace is earned.*
>
> **M. SCOTT PECK**

The first thing I've learned during my years of marriage to Alain LeNôtre, not to mention my emotional rollercoaster ride with the LeNôtre family, is that most of us have more than one calling. My callings to be a wife to Alain and to be a mother to my children are certainly fundamental ones in my life. What I now recognize as my most time-consuming calling, however, grew out of my day-to-day encounters with what our students needed.

By interviewing new recruits or scholarship applicants, talking them through problems, pointing them toward jobs as their studies with us neared an end, I found a new mission. I help students to get where they needed to be, to change their life, find a fulfilling career that enables them to feed their family and at the same time enjoy what they were doing. Sometimes students burst into tears in my office because of their marital troubles, or financial troubles and I console, advise and encourage them to the best of my abilities. And there are often nice surprises.

I remember in one of our first evening classes we had a sixty-year-old student who was undergoing chemotherapy though he'd been told that he had little chance of surviving cancer. Once he graduated, he retired to Galveston and opened his own restaurant by the bay, pinning his LeNôtre diploma on the entrance wall. He had miraculously recovered. I also remember a nineteen-year old girl who was raised in a dysfunctional family and when she enrolled in classes had a severe case of stuttering. During the course of her studies, she adopted our school as her own family, greatly improved her cooking skills, and got the class' best grades on the final exam! By then, her stuttering had disappeared. Everyone was amazed, students and chefs included.

There have been other rewarding experiences, like the student Drew Rogers who worked every day at a fulltime job but showed up evening after evening for our baking classes. After he graduated, he was able to open his own baking and pastry shop, hiring our students and graduates to help him manage and grow the place. He even made it on the Bakery Boss TV show! His pastry shop is thriving, and I am so proud of him.

What I also see among our students day after day is, quite frankly, a universe removed from the way Alain and I had grown up. I have talked with students working three jobs just to pay their bills, single mothers and single fathers, men and women without a true direction who hope the restaurant or pastry business might give them one.

But it was tuition that often was the most daunting roadblock for those seeking the education we offered. Something had to be done; yet, coming from the different world of France, where the universities are basically tuition-free, Alain and I initially had no idea what that was. Then, a member of our Culinary Institute Advisory Board, Houston-based corporate dining executive Randy Fournier, told us what we needed to do.

"You need a scholarship fund," Randy said. As I was looking at him skeptically, he continued. "You need to raise money to have a fund from which you can cover scholarships to help worthy students."

I nodded, unaware I was seeing my future.

"All the schools do it, large ones, small ones. All the universities especially. They do it all the time," he explained, "and they hire fulltime people to manage the fund."

"We certainly can't afford to hire anyone."

"That's why you'll have to do it yourself. And," Randy said, almost as an afterthought, "you'll just have to figure out how."

Remembering this conversation, it is remarkable how completely it defined my work for all the years since then. Yes, I had to set up a nonprofit, which I did first under the generic-sounding name Culinary Endowment and Scholarship. Still, after Alain's father passing, it became clearer to me that we had to honor him in a major way. After all, he had not only inspired Alain to enter the culinary world, but he had revolutionized the world Alain eventually entered. With the board's enthusiastic approval, I renamed the nonprofit Gaston LeNôtre Scholarship. It exists to this day, put forth primarily as an annual gala that raises funds toward helping Culinary Arts students of merit who need it most.

Still, my feelings for the students and prospective students I met each day ended up meaning that I felt compelled to help them in any way I could. I had chaired a gala a few years back for the Awty International School that our children attended. But that was easy enough. There was a development office with paid employees and, most importantly, very wealthy parents, who were willing to donate money and volunteer anytime. So yes, I had done this before. Yes, it was a big success, raising lots of money. But this new much-needed endeavor to be handled exclusively by me brought me a month of brooding and depressing thoughts all the same. Would I be able to do it, dreading mostly to ask people to donate.

By February of 2001, I had the administrative and legal parts of the foundation in place, and I started pushing myself into Houston's busy social whirl. I realized, even if slowly, that just as media coverage depended on establishing friendly relations with the media, raising money for a cause meant establishing friendly relations with people who had means.

I learned two things. First, it's much easier to play a role when you believe in it, as Alain and I believed in our ability to make our students lives better with education. And second, if you act friendly with people for an earnest cause, a fair number of them end up becoming your friends. Today, my list of leading donors and my list of close friends includes mostly the same names. The very people who support my mission have become my very best friends because I so appreciate what they do for our students, especially when they are constantly bombarded about important social, medical, art, or environmental causes.

Despite all the months of hard work required, a fundraising Gala certainly remains a labor of love. As of now, I have orchestrated a full dozen galas, including one in Kansas City to benefit Les Dames d'Escoffier, an organization of professional women who are leaders in the hospitality industry.

That first year, in 2001, we settled on a date. The gala would take place on Friday September 21. And as with all big events, that date produced a timeline showing when each thing had to be done. For instance, every gala needs to have a committee, honorary chairs, and chairs. I was lucky to meet Carolyn Farb at one of the French consul's receptions, and asked her, timidly or jokingly, if she would consider helping us by being our honorary chair! And she said yes. That gave me a boost. Carolyn proved very helpful and her book, *How to Raise Millions Helping Others Having a Ball,* is full of advice that I have used throughout the process. Things were coming together!

One of my favorite developments that first year involved our can-can dancers. At some point in our planning sessions the idea of having the traditional French entertainment at our gala came up, and everybody seemed for it. But nobody knew where, besides Paris, to find some can-can dancers. I got on the phone and called Houston Grand Opera, Houston Ballet, and the Alley Theatre—with no luck whatsoever. Finally my friend Katina McDannald gave me the right contact. Before long I had our can-can dancers. Everybody at our gala loved them so much, they became a recurring element year after year. I guess Texans never knew that the French have their version of hootin' and hollerin'.

By late spring, I began to make progress even in the hardest yet most important area of a fundraiser: funds. I remember meeting Katina and her husband Monty at a party, telling them about my fundraising project, and then finding their check in the mail a few days later. I could not help my tears rolling down my face. That was my first contribution. Everything was possible. Other checks followed, large and small, as the weeks turned into months. I began to feel this might actually work.

It's never easy talking to people about giving money. There are so many worthy and well-established charities in Houston— so many that there are several fundraising events or some sort of gala each night of each week. Houston is a city of much success, however, and perhaps, even more, of generosity.

And many individuals did sign on the dotted line, the highlight of our donation form. And without fail, they were true to their commitment, a testimony that Americans have a big heart.

The first Gala night, of September 21, 2001, drew closer, and then it was barely 10 days away. I had a theology class at the University of St. Thomas that Monday morning of September 11, and I was busily gathering my books and papers, getting ready in the room where Alain and Gaston were having breakfast and watching the morning news. But I was late and I had no time for anything like that. I glanced at the television, which was showing a pair of very tall buildings that were belching smoke. As I made it out the door, saying goodbye, I remember wondering what kind of film my husband and son were watching on such a bright Houston morning.

My professor set me straight when I joined everyone else in the classroom. We observed some silent moments for victims of the terrorist attacks on the World Trade Center in New York City and the Pentagon in Washington, D.C. Even as we spoke in somber tones, we did not yet have an understanding of how many were dying. As the information poured in, the tears in our classroom poured out. As everyone who witnessed these events understands, these were days of confusion and fear. If terrorists could strike once, they could strike more times, and maybe they could strike anywhere. People, for the most part, stayed home, partially mourning the loss of so many and partly, I think, hiding from whatever might happen to them.

We heard from some of our working graduates that restaurants were empty. People were fixing meals at home, using recipes they hadn't looked at in years; people were gathering their loved ones close. People were hugging each other, and people were crying. And I was planning an event that expected them to actually show up. It felt silly and meaningless, against such huge, historic events; yet that first gala was important, and there was still more work to do. When the country club offered to let us postpone without any financial penalty, I thought about it an hour or so but called them back.

"No," I said, "We need to go ahead with our Champagne & Chocolat Scholarship Gala."

That was what I'd named our gala by then, and that it remains.

There were a few additions to the program, of course. I remember looking out over the crowd, who showed up, nearly every one and hearing us all sing the National Anthem together facing the American flag. There were tears in many eyes, men right along with women. Alain and I could not have missed that oldest truth about America—he coming here from France, me coming here from Greece, and so many I could see coming here from so many places. When you come here, you become an American. You are America. And for all the politics of everyday life, you agree about more things than you disagree about. Starting with moments like this.

Our first gala was a success and a catharsis for us all. I could hear people telling each other that our event was their first night out since 9/11. And even though no one knew exactly what it would feel like, celebrating new hope in such circumstances, it quickly became clear that we all really needed that party. As with the deaths of our loved ones, we mourn everything that is lost. But we who remain must commit to living once again.

With my fellow dancers before a Greek concert at the Museum of Fine Arts Houston

With my parents and my three sisters, Neny, Elda, Athena.

CHAPTER 15

Do Not Apologize, You Were Fine

> *What you seek is seeking you.*
> **RUMI**

Few things in life help us focus our minds and hearts on what matters more powerfully than death—particularly the death of a parent, unless perhaps it's the deaths of both parents. It is the ultimate reminder that we are the grownups now, and that our own children look to us with the same needs, the same desires, the same questions we aimed at our parents. Having neither parent left alive is also a reminder that we are gifted with only so much time—time to love, time to create, and perhaps, especially, time to forgive. Yet of course, it's not the ones who've wronged us who truly seek or need our forgiveness. It is ourselves.

Through the same difficult period that Alain and I were growing the school and I was creating the nonprofit, I was forced to say goodbye to my parents back in Athens. Sometimes over the years, I might have wondered how this would be, how it might feel, based on the darkest of my thoughts about ways they had so often let me down, unknowingly for sure.

It was June 1, 1997, the Sunday morning after my parents

had celebrated their wedding anniversary with dinner in a Vouliagmeni restaurant. My sisters, Neny and Elda, who still lived there, had joined them. Now it was time to get ready for church. My father always went, my mother pretty much never, as she stayed home to cook the traditional Sunday meal. So on this particular Sunday, he shaved carefully, dressed in a nice suit, and started toward the kitchen door with the intention of saying goodbye to my mother. Instead, he fell back into a chair, calling her name, "Katie, Katie...," the victim of an aneurism.

Neny called me from Athens at 3 a.m. my time, with the news: "*O patéras mas péthane*. Papa is gone. It happened this morning. He went in peace, did not suffer." I felt not only shocked by my Father's sudden death, but I was also filled with regret. I had wanted to visit him over Easter that year. I'd had a sudden urge to go and spend a real Easter in Athens, as I used to do when I was a little girl, with my father, walking to church close to midnight, anticipating the Easter bells, so I could sing *Christos Anesti*, Christ has risen, over and over again, as loudly as I could.

In the end, my mother had talked me out of it.

"What's the use of coming at this time by yourself?" she said. "Stay with your husband and you'll come later in the summer as always. Don't leave your husband alone." To my mother, if you were a wife, you never left your husband alone. She knew what some husbands did when they were left alone. So I hadn't gone at Easter, and now that my father was dead, I tried to bury yet another resentment of just how I shouldn't have listened to my mother. Once again, I should not have listened to her. Well, it was too late now. I cried the rest of that long night.

Alain was tied up at the school, my two daughters at their universities, so my son Gaston and I traveled to Athens for the funeral. I wrote a little poem for the funeral speech, telling those gathered in the church how special my father had been to me. I shared how he took me outside into the fields, how he taught me to look at and smell the flowers in spring, how he'd reminded me to breathe strong and walk straight, and always to believe in the power of God.

At the end of the service, many relatives and family friends located me and confided to me how my father had helped them when they were in financial trouble, or maybe aided a struggling son or daughter. No one had ever told me of these Good Samaritan deeds, which had obviously shaped a good deal of his life. The picture of my father became more whole, and it pleased my heart. Contemplating his serene, slightly smiling face, my father looked like the late Pope John Paul II; I felt good. I knew he was at peace.

My mother lived fifteen more years after my father, essentially alone. To my relief, Neny and Elda remained in Athens and were able to at least check in on her, taking her for a meal outside or a walk on the seashore. One day, having reached the age of 92, my mother fell in her living room. She managed to call Elda and ended up safely in a hospital. But I can almost hear her doctor scolding her: "I told you to be careful not to fall." Her hip was twisted from the trauma, and considering the bones left weakened by osteoporosis, she never truly recovered. She spent two months in one rehabilitation center, two months more in another one, and her two final months in a wellness home.

Twice I flew to Athens, in March and May, and visited her, while there was still hope that she would survive. I was physically forcing her to move, to walk, to make the effort required to get better. And she was willing in the beginning, I felt; she liked me to be there, trying to feed her, to help her walk, to give her tea or applesauce. Ultimately she gave up. She was not motivated any longer. Eventually, she simply stayed in bed, my sisters said. She wouldn't move; she refused to talk, eat or drink anything.

My mother died on November 13, 2011, and I couldn't bring myself to go and see her in that very last month, as I knew she was so terribly diminished. I did not attend her funeral either. I didn't want to see my mother dead. I'm sure this was because I'd always hoped to have a real mother, one day, someone who would tell me all about herself as a woman, someone I could talk to, someone I belonged to, someone I knew. But my mother, I had to make her up in my *White Lamb* novel, out of bits of information that I could get from her or family members. This death was a double death for me—the death of my biological mother and the death of my wished-for mother. In the finality of this, I realized I'd never had a mother at all.

She left me without telling me a thing about herself and her life. The only words she kept repeating to me were "Enjoy yourselves as much as you can"—surely she knew what she meant. For me, I could not grasp that notion. But then again I was not a normal affectionate daughter either, I thought. I too had been keeping secrets from her ever since I was little. And I would even steal the chocolates she kept locked for guests—I always managed to find the keys.

At the end, though, when I had found out that she was close to death, I did ask her to forgive me, to forgive the bad daughter I had been as a teenager.

"Why," she said, quietly, "you should not apologize. You were fine."

As elusive and mysterious as she was, once she was gone, I missed my mother. As a little girl, I was cared for by different maids—distant relatives that my mother took under her wing for house help and compensated later by finding them a husband. But children crave motherly love and care. Living in the US for so long I have witnessed today's American mothers telling their children, even their grown children, I love you, love you baby, I love you sweetheart, I love you sweetie, I love you. They say it every day and sometimes several times a day. What a blessing.

My mother and father told me they loved me only a couple of times throughout my entire life. For sure they loved me, but their generation and culture were different, I suppose. I grew up unconsciously seeking validation from my parents. My mother would often tell me "You are beautiful," looking at me with admiration. As a young person, my impression was that she loved me only for my God-given looks. When later I managed to accomplish things not related to my looks and was trying to tell my mother my achievements on the phone, she seemed to not care whatsoever. I desperately wanted to tell her about my studies, my degrees, our culinary school, my charity work but she would only ask me questions about the family. "How is Nathalie, Armelle, Alain, Gaston, Cecile, Charles, Colette?"

I was proud to tell her about all that they did and accomplished, one by one. The truth is, by the time I was through telling her all about them, our conversation was over and done, and I was left with the bitter feeling of telling her nothing about myself, again. I wanted my mother to be proud of me for what I had accomplished. She certainly was, but I could not see or hear that. The fact that I had relinquished becoming a movie star always seemed to leave my mother disappointed with me, and there was nothing that I could do to change that, that's what it was always creeping in the back of my mind.

But maybe I am completely wrong. I was not able to see my mother's love and to feel it, and I was not able either to show her that I loved her no matter what. I was privileged to have a mother who did care for me and did her best.

For so many years, I've come to understand, I was seeking grace. A full sixteen years after reading and re-reading *The Road Less Traveled*, I set out to write about my own road. I prayed to God to help me write my book, but I didn't know what I really meant. Only now does it strike me, after the intense depression and humiliation I felt peeling back the layers to see myself evolving from these aloof states, struggling to express myself adequately, and to write a book with a profound message, that the message is something I carry within me. My purpose was not really to be a great writer, but to find grace and share it.

Because of the turn my young life took into the world of people I could not relate to, I had lost my connection with God. I became entangled in meaningless relationships that prevented me from achieving spiritual growth. I was swamped in stagnant waters for years, not fully enjoying my life as a woman, a mother, or a social being in either my family or my profession. I was lost in the dark, not proud of my empty life of my beginnings. My self-esteem was almost at zero, and I feared that this emptiness inside me had prevented me from giving my children what they needed to be the adults they were meant to be, exactly as my mother had failed to give me what I needed.

The truth is: I did not know what they needed and, even had I known, I had no clue where to find it within me. By studying psychology and psychotherapy along with other self-help books, and later with my spirituality in bloom, I gradually enlightened my mind and conscience. I do hope that my children have forgiven my failures and frailties, that they were able to transcend whatever I might have done but wasn't able to. I hope they will transmit better values and be loving, accepting parents themselves. I truly believe they have transcended, and I am so proud of all they've become.

Grace found me and saved me. But I had to do my part and travel the road of finding myself. This search has taken all the chapters of my life so far and surely will take the rest, but the most important thing is that I rediscovered my inner self, my soul, my spirit within. It took me years to finally have that glimpse, to find peace with myself, see all my shortcomings, mistakes, indulgences, laziness and resistance to do the work, endure the suffering, bear the pain, and finally accept it all. Now I want to hold onto that grace tightly and cherish it.

Finding grace is finding inner peace. This peace with ourselves creates room for the peace we long to have with all others. Finding grace is the first step to something larger, I've come to understand: it is the entrance to the realm of God.

Afterword

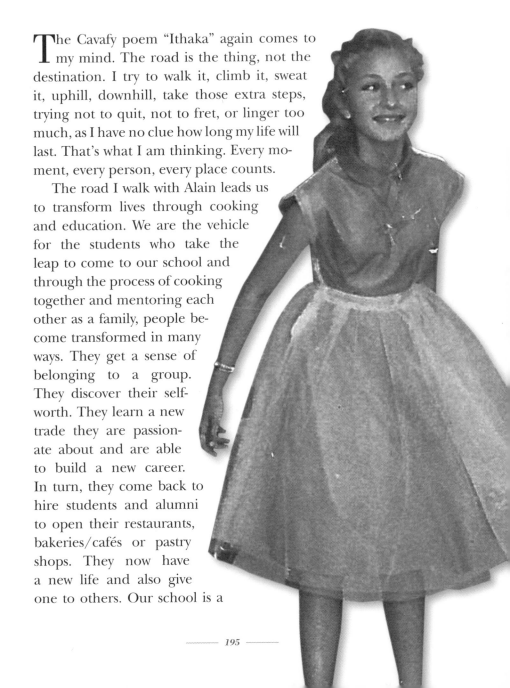

The Cavafy poem "Ithaka" again comes to my mind. The road is the thing, not the destination. I try to walk it, climb it, sweat it, uphill, downhill, take those extra steps, trying not to quit, not to fret, or linger too much, as I have no clue how long my life will last. That's what I am thinking. Every moment, every person, every place counts.

The road I walk with Alain leads us to transform lives through cooking and education. We are the vehicle for the students who take the leap to come to our school and through the process of cooking together and mentoring each other as a family, people become transformed in many ways. They get a sense of belonging to a group. They discover their self-worth. They learn a new trade they are passionate about and are able to build a new career. In turn, they come back to hire students and alumni to open their restaurants, bakeries/cafés or pastry shops. They now have a new life and also give one to others. Our school is a metaphor of rebirth and transformation, of giving and receiving, of using ones talents.

Our 2014 June-July summer course in Rome with the Franciscan fathers of the Atonement, put my life in perspective. The opportunity to revisit the many architectural splendors of Rome, its tall pine trees grazing the hills, along with the magnificent churches in every piazza and our excursion to the Etruscan tombs in nearby Lazio, made the experience a unique gift.

This trip was more than sightseeing. In addition to the tremendous reading materials, passionate discussions, and illuminating lectures in Inter-Religious dialogue and Ecumenism, there was a sense of community and communion with all the other students joining us from the US, Quebec, Colombia, Malta, Ethiopia and Italy. Walking every morning to the Centro Pro Unione in Piazza Navona, for our daily gatherings, I felt joy. Together with laity and priests, we transcended our obvious differences and created an *ecclesia*, a church.

The experience of bonding when one shares the same concerns, interests, and love for what is beautiful and universal, is essential to one's soul. I felt I cared for these people and told them so before departing. We all hugged afterwards, exchanging gifts. And it dawned on me that I've changed. I feel whole. I am able to give love to others because I feel love in myself. In the process of re-writing my life I stripped away the half-truths and emptied myself to discover who I am. And for that grace I am humbled and grateful.

Back in Corsica, in our summer family home, I am now closing up this memoir, gazing at the turquoise swaying waters of the Ajaccio Bay, the sailboats scattered around, and the planes from Napoleon Bonaparte airport, leaving their fluffy white mark in the sky. I am looking forward to flying to Athens at the end of the month to visit with my three sisters. Every year, a reunion with my sisters in my homeland is a pilgrimage and an emotional journey. I am eager to hug them and tell them I love you, because I have not in the past. They kept telling me they loved me, but I could not say it. I just couldn't.

This time I will. The truth is, it is the first time in my life that I have felt love for myself. Putting the last words in this memoir, I finally feel God's merciful love filling me up. I am able to hear, I love you Marie, I love you Marie, in all the languages I speak: *Σ αγαπώ, Je t'aime.* I love you Marie.

Ajaccio, August 1, 2014

*Alain in chocolate class at the LeNôtre
school in Plaisir, France*

In Their Own Words

CHEF DREW ROGERS, *Drew's Pastry Place*

When I turned 40, I had my own direct marketing business but it really wasn't my passion—it was just something I did. So my wife comes to me and says: If money and time were no object, what would you want to do? Well, I'm an Italian from New Jersey and I've always loved to cook and bake. I would, I decided, become a pastry chef. My wife started researching culinary programs behind my back, talked with Alain and Marie LeNôtre, and arranged for me to attend one of their open houses. When she saw the look on my face there, she said "You're going back to school." I wasn't a school person to begin with, but the instructors and chefs I learned from at LeNôtre were amazing. I'd come in early, stay late, and do whatever they asked in between. Mrs. LeNôtre was always nurturing, always positive.

After 50 weeks of going four nights a week, I graduated, and I went right to work as assistant pastry chef at Houston Country Club. I knew that was because of the LeNôtres, both because of what they taught me and the contacts they had. Almost four years later, my wife said it was time for me to open my own place. Which we did. That's how I ended up on Bakery Boss TV Show, after I'd been trying to get on another show from the Cake Boss people called The Next Great Baker. The show meant closing my place for nine days of filming—nine days edited down to 42 minutes. Since the show has aired, our business has gone crazy. In the beginning, we were six times over what we had been doing. And that has leveled out to three or four times.

Thanks to my background in Italian pastry like cannoli, that's really all I wanted to do at my shop. I wasn't the least bit interested in cupcakes, even though my wife kept telling me we could sell a bunch of them. I'd say: Any monkey can make cupcakes. It was on the show, right on national TV, that I had to admit my wife was right, and the idea of cannoli cupcakes came to me. I made up the recipe on the air, and I even trademarked the idea after that. Now we sell as many as 2,000 cannoli cupcakes on Fridays and Saturdays, and we sell a healthy number every other day. I do get a lot of grief from my fellow chefs, though. Come on, Drew, they say. Why'd you have to tell the whole world your wife was right?

CHEF MICHAEL GABRIEL, *BTG670*
For me, learning to cook at the LeNôtre School was a journey, a real struggle, mostly because of finances—as it is for a whole lot of the students there. I remember the first time I went to see the place, I had to put the whole thing off because I couldn't even afford the application fee, much less the tuition. Finally I got to start, with the help of a scholarship plus working around the school any way we could figure out how to let me. I became the purchasing chef there for the school, and then I worked in the restaurant, Kris Bistro. My involvement at LeNôtre was through-out. I even became captain of the school's culinary competition team. Everything for me came from the school. They gave me the guidance I needed in my career. And once I had that, I just ran with it.

I started at Culinary Institute LeNôtre in 2009 and graduated in 2011, with both a culinary arts degree and a culinary man-agement degree. I loved LeNôtre so much because it was the only French culinary school around here that had real French instructors teaching real French techniques. The classes were small and hands-on, so that I didn't have to fight against so many things just to gain knowledge. After I graduated, I started my private chef business, and then got a job as head chef in an as-sisted living facility. I even got to compete on TV's Hell's Kitchen. And now I've opened my own food truck called BTG670 serving foods of the Pacific Islands, since my wife is from Saipan.

We are roasting 150-pound pigs whole in the truck. I want to bring the island feel to that, since that's what took me on this journey in the first place. I want to provide a life for my kids. The main thing I learned from LeNôtre was the techniques, right along with the respect for what you do. I gained a whole new level of respect for chefs and for this field. Everybody changes the ingredients, but everybody does the same basic technique. If you've been taught to prepare things properly, you can change the ingredients all day long.

CHEF DAVID DENIS, *LE MISTRAL restaurant*

Falling between when I quit working as a private chef to an affluent Houston family and when I opened my own restaurant called Le Mistral, the nine months I spent as a chef-instructor at the LeNôtre School were the perfect transition. It was a great experience for me. And with different classes throughout the day—morning, afternoon and evening—there was some time for me to work on my business plan and my designs for the restaurant. Both Alain and Marie were very supportive of my contributions to the school, and also of my "moonlighting" toward Le Mistral. They definitely appreciated that I was an entrepreneur.

I quit being a private chef because I got mad. My mother and grandmother, both of whom taught me so much about cooking back in the South of France, came to Houston for Christmas. And at the last minute, the family I cooked for decided to go to California and made me go with them. I thought: this has to stop. I heard about Alain LeNôtre building this culinary institute and I heard about their education director, a French chef named Jacques Fox. I remember coming to the school and the first guy I bump into is Jacques. You know Jacques: you're going to like this guy. We really clicked for each other. It wasn't long, teaching at LeNôtre, before we started planning the restaurant that became Artisans.

Jacques told me I could have a job, but then I had to go meet Mr. and Mrs. LeNôtre. I learned that Alain is very focused and business like. But Marie—after thirty minutes we'll have talked about all kinds of things. Alain kept laughing at the way our conversation wandered. "Don't talk so much to my wife," he said, pushing the joke to the next level. "I am a very jealous man."

The school was great. I really liked the organization. I like the

With legendary Chef Julia Child

students having hands-on cooking instruction, not just sitting around talking about food. In terms of French cuisine, it was very basic stuff, but it was the most important stuff. I knew exactly what the students learned in my classes, and I knew the ones that learned it best. When I opened Le Mistral, the first small version, I hired four or five LeNôtre students to open it with me. And when I bought land and started construction on today's 11,000-square foot Le Mistral, Alain and Marie were among the first to come take a look. I remember Marie gazing up as the building came together and smiling. "You're crazy," she said. "Just like us."

Poetry

Poem song I wrote to Alain, in French in 1980, the year we met.

TU ES MA DESTINÉE

Tu es ma destinée, mon âme, ma conscience
C'est toi ma source, ma finalité
Je t'aime tous les jours dans le temps dans l'espace
Je t'aimerai toujours et pour l'éternité

J'ouvrirai ma mémoire et je te raconterai
Des milliers d'histoires que personne ne connaît
J'ouvrirai le ciel et tu découvriras
Cet astre éternel ou tu t'accrocheras

And, here is my English translation:

You are my destiny, my soul, my conscience
You are my source and my finality
I love you every day in time and space
I will love you forever and for eternity

I will open my memory and recount to you
A thousand stories that no one ever knew
I will open the skies and you will discover
The everlasting star that you will hang on to

A selection of poems written in 1993-1994 in Houston

ANGEL SONG

I will grow into an angel
I will grow into a tree
I'll become a pure maple.
I'll become a manuscript.

If you let me see your rainbow
I will draw you a million stars
If you let me feel your sorrow
I will give you joy in bars.

I will feed you, I will pull you
To the sun, your prime source
I will hug you, and then escort you
To the Lord, in heaven gloss.

I will grow into an angel
I will grow into a tree
I'll become a pure maple.
I'll become a manuscript.

PERAMA

Her house was small and white
Amid peach and apricot trees
In Perama. To go there

One had to cross the sea, somewhere
From Piraeus by ferry boat
The car inside, I crossed my past.

Eleni was my nanny
Years ago, in Athens.
She hadn't changed at all.

Same red face like a pumpkin
And the smile ample, shiny
A whole world.

She cleaned my diapers and fed me
When mother was elsewhere,
having a good time.

She loved me, she said,
With her tiny brown eyes.
A copper tin she gave me

And a gold chain. Her husband
Scrawled farewell words for me
In a bottle of ouzo.

Perama! This is the place
Where she lives today, in Greece.
How could I forget?

THE SKY IS NEAR

My friend I told you some years ago
When we both met at chez Caspar's
That I will show you a world of awe
A world of lights and thousand stars

My friend I told you to sweep your anguish
Assets and favors and quit the show
And climb the hills, those scary mountains
And see the sky from there above

Now is the moment we so much longed for
You and your family, me and my fears
Now come the splendors, now come the tears
Believe my friend, the sky is near

EVE

Here I am
Fragile and bare
Yet in winter I can subsist
And in the spring
With the sun's care
I'll bloom a flower
I'll make a feast

Here I am
Rejoice and hope
And hold my arm
And be my friend
For I can promise
I will adore you
For ever more
And with no end

MELANCHOLY

I walked along the banks
Of **La Seine** *river*
Then sat on a bench
That faced **Notre Dame**

How beautiful she was
I though, and smiled
Even if old and grey
She was majestic

I saw my life
Travel slow
Like that old boat
Which caught my eye

It passed the church
Made few waves
Then got shadowy and small
Faded away

I looked at Notre Dame
Again and thought
How beautiful she was,
How Majestic

THE BICYCLE

The bicycle takes me
To my aunts' abode
Where the fire is burning
And the food is hot

The bicycle guides me
To my closest friend
She knows how alone
I can be, how damn cold

I stay there for a few weeks
To warm my inner most soul
I gain strength, I grow old
I breathe again the wind

And here I am, again
Riding my weary dear bicycle
Here I am, pedaling wild
Heading to the sun's beam

EMBRACED BY THE WIND

The giving up of the self
As if the self were no longer
But married to the cosmos

Like the grain of sand is
Amid billions of grains of sand
Embraced by the wind, the flow.

ADAM

He traces heavens, he makes up stars
Absurd, bigot, stubborn, somewhat
Man is a man, is a man, is a man.

Man is a terror when he dares
To seek for light in huge despair
He traces heavens, he makes up stars

Don't be misled, he is often nice
To his fellow humans, when he can
Man is a man, is a man, is a man.

A pure, authentic, godly device
Once he transcends himself he glows
He traces heavens, he makes up stars

Ingenious despite his flaws. Yet
Enraptured by notoriety, he blows up
Man is a man, is a man, is a man.

Man is a beast, a cryptic soul
Don't ever judge him, you'll be vulgar
He traces heavens, he makes up stars
Man is a man, is a man, is a man.

THE TUNNEL

This is the end
Of the black tunnel

I see the light
I smell the trees

I find my voice
I hear the bees

And now my friend
Look at my pallor

Look at my body
Look at my face

You recognize the one
You once dreamt for?

Will we prevail?
Will then embrace?

THE TINY FLOWER

A pink flower, smaller
Than a shirt button
Hangs on the top
Of my kalanchoe plant

It stands still, leaning
Towards the lofty window
Where the day' light
Spreads from above.

And I stare
Dazed and colorless
Facing my plastic
Blue computer screen

I stare and think
How tiny, how small
This pink flower is
And yet it bears all

THE GRAND CANYON

Along the South Rim trail
We walked for about two hours
Then sat under the sun facing the Canyon.

A ranger, beard, uniform and boots
Gave us a talk on the origins
Of the Colorado River
The old one and the new,
The red river and also
The endangered river,

The history of the rock,
Sandstone, mudstone, limestone,
Millions of years old.
Alain remarked, Teilhard de Chardin
Explained all this
In the "Vision of the Past".

And I reflected heavily upon
Teilhard's theory as we walked back
Marveled by the giant sculpted rocks,

All shades of read
Orange, ochre, grey,
Contrasting with the green of the trees.

At one o'clock, I got hungry.
All the red rock reminded me of red meat,
The limestone, fettuccini alfredo,

And the pines, crispy lettuce,
French green beans.
Metaphysics were out of my mind. Then,

Alain stopped staring at the ground.
Legs on the top of a hole,
A black tarantula blocked the entrance

To another one of her species
Identical, paralyzed in a vertical position
On the brink, by the first one's two legs.

My god, it seems like hard sex, I said.
My dear, said he, it's clearly a war scene.
Enemies can't live under the same roof.

I threw a pebble and waited
But nothing moved
My hunger for food had disappeared.

GLIDING

The moment you realize your smallness
You enter miraculously
The kingdom of consciousness

Because you are nothing
You are everything
You are the star and the parcel of dust
You are the woman the man the good and evil

And now you don't panic
You accept
You behold
You glide…

JUST BE

I let myself be, just be
No need to become something
No fear to be only me
I let myself be, just be

Be part of the happening
The everyday wonder
A vehicle of God's will
A plain whole human being

I let myself be, just be

BERRIES

Rain fell all night. Wind
froze the bricks. At dawn, berries,
red, loaded the trees.

PAUL

"English, English, English,
Speak English, if you want
To be heard here, in this town,"

Said the man who drove a blue
Pickup and drank a coke. "In fact
What new thing you have to say?

We know everything we need up here.
Look at the sky, it's going to rain
And you can do nothing about that."

Of course, I said, of course
I'll walk away. There is nothing
To say more that is was my pleasure

Meeting one of you. You look
Gentle and tanned, healthy,
Civilized and all that.

But what do you do when it rains?
Do you work? Stand still and wait?
Or watch amazed the works of God?

Do you believe, or not?
Are you Paul? I think I saw you once
Or was it not you? Who are you?"

The man shut off the engine, numb.
His beard turned white, his eyes red.
This sky cleared then, sun rays appeared.

HAPPY BIRTHDAY!

Happy Birthday dear You!
A year has gone full of surprises and wins
I bet our days of enlightenment
Are not yet over

My gift for you lies in my hips
That bears for ever my passion's tips
And in my lips which never shut, but

Dazzling, brighten the days afar
Do not forget the blond hair though
That grows for you only and blows
All subtle discontents, all future bores

I won't refer yet to my heart
Which never stops, marking the fact
That ceaseless love is my sole aim

Besides, here, inside my skull
Billions of neurons serve that plan
And right now they are in process
To stamp my fervor for eternity

DEAFNESS A CULTURE

In a sense, a new "ethnic" group has emerged in this country;
the deaf. They see their condition as a cultural identity
and they don't want to be "fixed".
The Atlantic Monthly—September 1993

Part of the group I am for sure
And I don't want to be fixed.
It doesn't matter that I'm Greek,
My most ethnic particularity
Is the deaf thing, and I wouldn't
Prefer to be able to hear.

Advances in genetic engineering led
To a cochlear implant to transform my life,
With a wire in my inner ear, plus
A tiny receiver under my skin
to hear ordinary conversations like
Barking dogs and honking cars?

Is this a miracle of biblical
Proportions to make the deaf hear?
Deafness is not a deprivation.
My soul will be altered by a new device.
Mainstreaming would mutilate me.

I don't want to hear, ever
Or answer the phone, polite,
And listen to some silly talk
Go to PTA meetings and lunches,
or do self-promoting charity work.

I don't want to be cured or
Speak and act like everybody does.
Uniquely disable, heterogeneous, deaf
I am once and for all.
Can't you hear?
I don't want to be fixed at all.

INVOLVING TRUST

Involving trust, Beth said,
You just trust yourself.

And I wrote that down carefully.
And I thought, damn it, is this a connivance

To get my words out
And prevent me from being peaceful?

Just do it, Bill said, trust the God within.
Yea, just do it, is easy to say.

To wake me up from torpor
I'd need a genuine slapping.

In deep sleep, my sight has gone, vanished.
Where is my energy, my faith?

Steadfast, she said
I bet I need to be in control of my hopes.

I breathe in, yet forget to breathe out.
Is this my quest? Trust, Breathe out, Write it down?

"Forever a woman" was the title of a book I started.
Two chapters I wrote, and then, no more.

The book was supposed to tell my story, a bit,
Because my story cannot be told in one piece

But in a little bits. And so it goes. I make poems.
Mark said, it's beautiful what you write,

I love it. Maybe I am useful after all
And spread benevolence. Betty said,

You brought positive energy to the group!
Yes, I am useful, like the light.

Just turn me on, damn it, don't forget to turn me on.
Someone needs to be there to turn me on,

To put me on fire, to make me the fire,
The Vestal goddess
The one who guards the fire burning, always,
Always, alive in the sanctuary.

Involving trust, she said
And I knew why I came there.

Promenade Gaston Lenôtre

(1920 - 2009)

Maître - Pâtissier

Colette LeNôtre stands in front of the sign honoring Gaston LeNôtre in the park in Bernay where they were married.